THE
KNOWLEDGE MANAGER

adding value in the information age

Steve Morris
John Meed
Neil Svensen

London · Hong Kong · Johannesburg
Melbourne · Singapore · Washington DC

PITMAN PUBLISHING
128 Long Acre, London WC2E 9AN
Tel: +44 (0)171 447 2000
Fax: +44 (0)171 240 5771

A Division of Pearson Professional Limited

First published in Great Britain in 1996

The right of Steve Morris, John Meed and Neil Svensen
to be identified as authors of this work has been asserted by them
in accordance with the Copyright, Designs and Patents Act 1988.

ISBN 0 273 62535 7

British Library Cataloguing in Publication Data
A CIP catalogue record for this book can be obtained from the British Library.

10 9 8 7 6 5 4 3 2

Typeset by Northern Phototypesetting Co. Ltd, Bolton
Printed and bound in Great Britain by Bell & Bain Ltd, Glasgow

The Publishers' policy is to use paper manufactured from sustainable forests.

about the authors

STEVE MORRIS

Steve Morris is Managing Director of the Burton Morris Consultancy, based in London. A consultant writer and researcher, he has worked extensively with a range of top global companies, including Visa International. He is the author of a number of best-selling management books, amongst them *How to Lead a Winning Team* and *Connecting With Your Customers*. His particular interest lies in how to address the challenge of working out communication strategies in the light of the Information Revolution.

JOHN MEED

John began work with the Audio Visual Media Research Unit of the Open University, before moving on to join the National Extension College in Cambridge, where he became Assistant Director for Education. John is now a partner in Learners First, a new organisation devoted to researching key educational issues, and to developing open and flexible learning materials. John has two children, and his interests include pop music, walking, reading, cinema and eating.

NEIL SVENSEN

Neil Svensen is founder and Managing Director of Rufus Leonard, a central London design agency whose clients include Visa International, the BBC and Shell International. He also works as a consultant for a number of large companies worldwide. His designs have been archived at the Victoria & Albert Museum and he has a special interest in new communications media.

acknowledgements

The authors would like to thank Paul Grover who wrote the sections on Understanding the language and the glossary.

We would also like to thank the managers who gave their time to us to talk about the new world order and their part in it.

contents

introduction

■ About this book

Welcome to this book about the information age. We wanted it to be different from other books on the information age.

Why?

Because we don't much like the other books on the information age. We don't like them because they are rabid, overrevved, and frankly annoying.

They make big assumptions and they are difficult to read – either full of complicated jargon or run mad with hype. To be honest, we find most of the material written about the information age to be a waste of good trees. And we like trees.

We didn't want our book to be a waste of trees.

We wanted it to be about the information age and the managers who will live through it. We wanted to help real managers deal with real issues and problems. We wanted to ground it in some kind of reality so that when you read it you feel that it relates to you, is of interest to you, and indeed of some help.

It was while traveling along this road that we decided upon the idea of getting some real managers to tell us some real stories about themselves. So this book has a selection of "letters" from people whom we believe are pretty typical of those living through this undoubted revolution. We didn't interview the great and the good. We just interviewed regular managers.

And another thing – we *are* excited by what is happening and what will continue to happen. But we didn't want to come over all preachy. We believe that the world is changing fast and that these are exciting times to live in.

We also believe that the information age, while important, will leave many things untouched. People will still be born, live, and die. People will still find more trouble at work in dealing with awkward people than they will in mastering how to use spreadsheets. E-mail will not mean an end to face-to-face contact.

■ Before we start

Before we launch into the book, there are three observations to get us started.

Hold onto your hats, folks

This book is about change. It is about the increasingly fast pace of change that has heralded in the information age. In fact, the pace of change can seem positively frightening.

If the technology in the car industry had changed at the same rate as in the computer industry you could buy a top of the range Rolls-Royce car for just over £1.50. The car itself would travel comfortably at the speed of sound and would do a round trip to Manchester on a thimbleful of fuel.

> If the technology in the car industry had changed at the same rate as in the computer industry you could buy a top of the range Rolls-Royce car for just over £1.50.

And that's just where we are now. You can't avoid change and in this new information age it will, at the very least, affect the kind of work we do and how we do it. That is for sure.

If there ever was a war

If like the authors of this book you are a Cold War baby, then the fear of war may well be with you.

But even war is likely to change as a result of the information age. Countries now plan for war fought not by soldiers but by computers. The new weapon is likely to be a Trojan horse planted inside an enemy's system. War will be over before it begins.

In an article in the London *Daily Telegraph*, writer Christy Campbell explains that the US military believes the next big war may be fought as an information war.

American officials believe that more than 120 governments are developing techniques for crippling enemy defenses by disrupting their computers. We could have an infowar with the aim being to destroy the stock exchange or the banking infrastructure.

A White House panel has warned that:

> A strategic attack against the US could be prepared under the guise of unstructured hacker activity.

A team is working on infecting enemy computer systems with software viruses that will stay dormant unless the weapon system is used against the US. And this is where it starts to get really interesting.

American officials believe that more than 120 governments are developing techniques for crippling enemy defenses by disrupting their computers.

The US military realized it had to get smart if it was to fight an infowar. It needed to absorb more about the infoworld. It needed to get used to handling lots of information in an electronic format and to making crucial decisions based upon it.

So a high-ranking colonel went with a group of senior officers to the New York Trade Center to see how commodities traders made split-second decisions as they scanned up-to-the-minute electronic data. It was a vast culture shock. The military was used to silent offices and people passively taking orders. On the floor it was loud, fast, difficult to follow. It was information overload. But the commodities dealers could handle the information and do something with it. The military was easily outdone amid the din and the volume of information.

The military then invited the traders to play their computerized wargame. The traders picked it up much quicker than the soldiers did in their world. As Colonel Tom Harkins said:

"They (the traders) have a technique for rapid pattern analysis that is world class."

Since then the military has learned from the traders and new skills have been developed. But the story is interesting. You may not need to work in the mad world of a dealing house, but you do need to develop similar world-class skills of analyzing data and turning it into useful information.

The knowledge manager

So it is that we approach the start of the book. And we believe that the book is well-named. The manager who succeeds in the information age will understand that we need to move from simple data (of which there is a mountain of the stuff), to information (of which there is a mountain) to knowledge (of which there is still sadly little). The art and the science of the information age will be for managers to gain intelligence, to turn information and data into knowledge that helps push themselves and their organizations onwards and upwards.

Knowledge and intelligence come from information, but they take it on and are the new genuine building blocks of the information age. It is knowledge that will lead to new products, new innovations and a business that genuinely offers a one-to-one service to customers. And despite all the machinery at the heart of this new age it is managers and their ability to turn information into knowledge that will be a company's greatest asset.

A gaze into the future

Just a quick gaze into the future before we begin.

Even now we can see data in a graphical way. We can visualize data using three-dimensional programs. The office of the future may allow us to hit a touch pad and see a map of where information is.

The new challenge for organizations will be in the form of data-mining. Getting out all that precious information from the avalanche that is already there. And as the computers and the software get more sophisticated then it is the miners that will inherit the earth. Whereas before the mining was for coal and minerals, the new miners will search for information. They will be aided by neural networks (computer programs that learn) and intelligent agents (electronic helpers on the information super-highway) and really sophisticated search tools and engines.

> Today's organization needs to turn all the information available into knowledge.

But the horny handed sons and daughters of toil of the new information revolution will not be brushing coal dust from their faces. They will be plugged in and ready to go.

Have fun

Today's organization needs to turn all the information available into knowledge. We look at this later on, but it is worth mentioning here because it is one of the main themes of the book.

Organizations need to learn and keep learning. And if we live in an information-rich environment then the need for effective sharing is important.

So it is now time to embark on an exploration of the information age. Have fun.

Feedback

If readers have any comments or suggestions regarding this book then please e-mail the authors at the following address:
email:feedback@rldesign.co.uk

YOU SAY YOU
WANT A
REVOLUTION?

- Is there really an information revolution?

- How does it feel?

- Bankable cornerstones

- The new hunter gatherers – or the rise of the
  information champion

Could information be
becoming the new means of
production, replacing capital
and land before it?

Is there really an information revolution?

1968. Revolution is in the air. The cobble stones of Paris have become barricades. The Prague Spring is flowering. Western young people are demonstrating against the Vietnam war.

1968. The Beatles release the *White Album*. Side four track one is appropriately called "Revolution"– a suitable title for turbulent times. But John Lennon's lyric is not a call to the barricades. Instead he comments sceptically:

> "But if you go carrying pictures of Chairman Mao
> You ain't gonna make it with anyone anyhow …"

John Lennon,
"Revolution"

Thirty years on, and Lennon's skepticism looks well founded. True, De Gaulle did not stay on as President – but it was another 13 years before a distinctly nonrevolutionary socialist government came to power in France. True, the tanks left the streets of Prague – but over 20 years later. True, the students blew their minds – but they returned to campus, thence to become the captains of industry. It's hardly been a revolution.

And yet, listen. … There are voices that would have us believe that revolution is still in the air. Here's one of them:

> Information technology is altering everything. It is causing the most significant change in the way we organise, live, make war, and do politics in a thousand years. The world has been turned upside down and the computer, along with telecommunications networks, is the engine of the revolution.

Tom Peters,
Liberation Management

And John Maxwell Hamilton talks of:

> … a technological revolution that is shaping our lives as profoundly as the industrial revolution in the 19th century reshaped the lives of our forebears.

John Maxwell,
Hamilton,
Keeping up with Information

No one would argue that there have been some pretty radical changes over the last 20 years. But is it really a revolution? Who might shed some light on the question?

Possibly the most important writer on revolutions has been Karl Marx. Marx argued that revolutions arose from conflict between classes around what he called the "means of production," or wealth generation. One class – the dominant class owned the means of production and exploited those who did not.

In the mediaeval period, the principal means of production was land, while in the capitalist period it was capital. In the eighteenth and nineteenth centuries revolutions were provoked as the owners of land gave way to the owners of capital.

As the owners of capital became the new dominant class – the "bourgeoisie" – so they in turn became the oppressors of the working class. As each class held such profoundly different interests this must inevitably, in Marx's view, lead to revolution and the eventual demise of capitalism, and the emergence of a new, class- and capital-free era.

Marx's analysis of historical development is profound, even though his predictions for the future have not materialized. The emergence of factors such as colonialism and the north–south divide, and the ability of capitalism to transmute and adopt new, more acceptable guises, were all largely unforeseeable at the time Marx was writing, and contributed to his getting at least some of it wrong.

But could Marx have been *this* wrong? Could information be becoming the new means of production, replacing capital and land before it? Could information itself be driving the next revolution? Alvin Toffler argues that it is. He talks of:

The rise of a new power system replacing that of the industrial past.

Alvin Toffler,
*Powershift:
Knowledge,
Wealth and
Violence at the
Edge of the 21st
Century*

while Drucker adds:

> Knowledge now has become the capital of a developed economy.

Peter Drucker,
*The New
Realities*

If information is indeed becoming the new means of production, what might we expect to happen? Following Marx's model, we might expect a new breed of information champions to emerge and challenge the dinosaurs of capitalism. Fleet of foot and mobile of modem they would rapidly gain ownership of the new means of production and acquire dominance.

They would in turn seek to oppress those without information. A new divide would open between the "info rich" and the "info poor," to use Haywood's terms, with two new classes having contradictory interests, and destined to conflict.

What evidence might support such a claim?

Certainly, we have witnessed the decline of some of the traditional capital-intensive industries, and the emergence of new, leaner organizations. More and more of the workforce now operates in the service sector, and services are the fastest growing areas of the economy. The thirst for capital in these new organizations is much less than in the manufacturing sector – and the thirst for knowledge may be greater. And many people are puzzled as the manufacturing base dwindles, yet the economy refuses to collapse – is this evidence of the declining influence of capital?

As Drucker argues, we have seen capital centered increasingly in the hands of pension companies rather than the classic capitalists of the nineteenth century. Increasingly decision making has moved from the owner to the manager, and now down or out to the "knowledge workers" who are in increasing demand.

> We believe that … in recent decades most of the emphasis has been on information technology rather than information. We are about to see a fundamental shift to wider consideration of information, knowledge and wisdom, with IT positioned as an enabling factor.

Geoffrey
Darnton
and Sergio
Giacoletto,
*Information in
the Enterprise:
It's more than
Technology*

How does it feel?

So how do we know we're in some kind of revolution? One of the main reasons is this: because the world feels and is different – in several very important ways.

> The pattern of work in the industrialized world has radically changed. Take the 1960s. Half of the workers in the industrialized world were involved in some way in making things. By the year 2000, not one developed country will have more than 13 per cent of people working in making things. The whole basis of the economy has changed.

■ The balance of resources has changed

Well one of the ways we know is that there are old notions about the world that no longer fit. And it's here we can see definite proof that we're entering a new kind of age. In the industrial age we believed that there were four main business resources, the famous four *M*s. These were men (*sic*), machines, materials, and money. But today this looks awfully thin. For one thing, half the population is missing. For another, we now have a fifth key ingredient – information.

In the industrial age we believed that there were four main business resources, the famous four *M*s: men, machines, materials, and money. But today this looks awfully thin.

And this, of course, means that we need to start to treat information as a resource. And while we've always looked at information as being rather passive and inconsequential, as something to be controlled and marshalled, now we need to look at it again.

What makes it rather interesting is that traditionally resources have been scarce and this of course has pushed the price up and put them at a premium. But information isn't scarce at all. It's everywhere and the real new challenge we face is to actually synthesize it, use it, and make the most of it.

And what's more, information is intangible. It's hard to say where it's stored and it's desperately unpredictable. This means we need to find a new way of looking at business and we only need to do this if we can accept that we genuinely are in the middle of radical change.

> We need to start to treat information as a resource.

■ Jobs have changed

Another sign that we're in a revolution is that it changes the way that we work. Any revolution worth its salt has been about change. Often revolutions have been driven by the chronic and overpowering need to sweep away an old order. And again here the information revolution is interesting. It is not as if it has suddenly come from nowhere, from a burst of anger. It has gradually built up, almost stealthily taking us by surprise. But it is here, and our jobs as managers are quite different as a result.

Today, every business is an information business and every manager is an information manager – or knowledge manager as the TSB (a bank in the UK) now calls its employees.

So we need to understand that all of us are now going to be information managers. At the most basic level, this means that we're going to need to get to grips with information technology (IT) – every job will have an element of IT in the future.

But this is merely the tip of the iceberg. Managers will be measured in the future by how they can use the information creatively, how they can synthesize it.

Many jobs will cease to exist. Many administrative posts will be redundant as machines continue to take over work previously done by people. But there will be an explosion of jobs in system support.

■ Organizations have changed

And this creates a challenge. It's been all too easy over the last ten years to see only certain rather high-tech businesses as information businesses, and the managers within them as information managers.

Airlines like British Airways have become paradigms in the business press for using their relationship databases, collecting information on customers, and using it to help them drive the business. But these days information as a key commodity and driver of the revolution has spread well beyond these initial early bounds. You're as likely to find a hospital in the state sector or a pharmaceutical company seeing itself as being in the business of information as you are an airline, a bank or a credit card company.

Another reason we know we're in a revolution is that information itself is helping to shape the way we see things. It's actually allowing us to develop new products and services, and to define businesses in new ways.

■ And it's going to go on changing

It's a characteristic of revolutions that the models – the ways of looking at the revolution, the ways of helping us come to terms with it – tend to lag far behind the revolution itself. And here things are no different. As the world moves on apace we're left with some rather flimsy ways of coming to terms with it.

In chapter three we'll look in more detail at some of the models and try to help people to see the pattern that's emerging, but it is fair to say that there are some things we can actually can predict.

This is how Professor Michael J. Earl, Andersen Consulting Professor of Information, describes what we are likely to see.

Michael J. Earl

"Scenarios are likely to include a shift from organizational hierarchies to multilevel networks, from bounded to virtual organizations, from decision making by numbers and analysis to decision making by exploration and creativity, from work based on physical action to time spent on intellectual reflection, from programmed and orchestrated endeavours to business experiment and rapid change, from national and local context to global and sibus faced."

As Professor Earl points out in his article in *Mastering Management*, the models will need to develop quickly to keep pace with the revolution that's overcoming us.

He also makes the interesting observation that yesterday's entrepreneurs will be replaced by "infopreneurs." It's these people that will make the most of the information and are likely to be up there pioneering their way around the world.

And how do we know we're in a revolution? Well it's going to change everything. Douglas Adams, author of the *Hitchhikers Guide to the Galaxy* has said,

> "We're going to be in a sea of communication, affecting the way we work, think, order pizza."

Douglas Adams,
author

■ Ordinary life may change

Look around your living room and you are likely to see a TV set, hi-fi, and a range of other electronic bits and pieces. The home of the future is likely to change quite significantly. There is every chance that the way we receive and transmit information will become one device. So the phone, PC, television, audio equipment, and maybe more, are likely to be in one box.

So our homes may look different in the years to come.

Also where we now have a garage or shed we may also have a small box outside the home which stores on disk all our music, films, and other entertainment.

The internal "architecture" of our daily lives will undoubtedly change.

And our work patterns may change to match. There is bound to be more homeworking, for instance. We are bound to shop from home more regularly through virtual supermarkets.

So we should notice changes in our everyday lives.

Bankable cornerstones

So what does the revolution – or at least the profound change – look like? What are the bankable cornerstones?

■ The new equation – t≠id²

Let's start with some figures. How about this?

- In 1500 you couldn't send a parcel to Australia – you wouldn't have known it existed.
- In 1900 you could send a parcel to Australia – but it would take three weeks to get there.
- In 1960 you could use air mail – allow a week.
- In 1996 you can send it by fax, e-mail, electronic file transfer – and it's there in minutes or even seconds.

Until now, there was a simple equation. It took a day to send a piece of information 300 miles. Send it 600 miles, it might take two days. Send it 3,000 miles and you'd need at least a week. Pay more and you could tamper with the equation – but you couldn't change it. The greater the distance (d), the more the information (i), the more time (t) it took: $t=id^2$.

The incredible shrinking world

Take the humble debit card. Walk into a record shop in downtown Outer Mongolia, pick up a CD and present your piece of plastic. The message from the electronic terminal zips through to your bank in Boston, via the shopkeeper's bank, through a data-processing center, possibly in the UK. In just six seconds your account has been scanned to find out whether you have the cash to pay, a sophisticated neural network computer has activated an antifraud program to check whether a fraud is likely, and then the money has been debited from your account. Yes, in just six seconds you can leap the globe. Possible a journey spanning tens of thousands of miles over computer and 'phone. If it wasn't called science, we would call it magic.

And what makes this so incredible is that the first Visa card, for instance, was only introduced in the 1970s.

Now the equation has changed. Distance has ceased to matter, and has virtually dropped out of the equation. Information can move at breathtaking speed around the planet.

> Until now there was a simple equation. It took a day to send a piece of information 300 miles. Send it 600 miles, it might take two days. Send it 3,000 miles and you'd need at least a week.

When the Nazis opened concentration camps in eastern Europe, it took a remarkably long time for hard information to reach the allies. Rumors filtered through, eyewitness accounts reached Einstein in the US, but it was not until the Russians arrived in the camps that the full horror of the holocaust became apparent.

When concentration camps appeared in Bosnia, the world's media was there within days. Detailed, validated eyewitness accounts emerged at once.

> One can question whether the world's response to the information from the Bosnian crisis was sufficiently quick, resolute, or effective. One cannot question that the information was there to act on in time.

One can question whether the world's response to the information from the Bosnian crisis was sufficiently quick, resolute, or effective. One cannot question that the information was there to act on in time.

This is the first bankable cornerstone – a new equation. Here are some examples of how it is affecting businesses around the world:

Soho-based film effects company Cinesite has installed state-of-the-art equipment which enables them not only to receive rushes, create special effects and transmit finished work digitally but to conduct daily transatlantic conferences with creatives in London and LA.

Reported in *Wired*, March 1996

Texas Instruments has sites across the world, including the US, Australia, Europe, South America, and the Pacific. Leasing satellite channels has enabled it to develop a dedicated communications system to exchange information such as designs between sites. An increasing proportion of design work can now be done from home offices.

(Adapted from John Maxwell Hamilton, *Keeping up with the Information*)

It has been estimated (Pritchett, 1994) that a weekday edition of the London *Times* newspaper contains more information than the average person in seventeenth century England came across in a whole lifetime. And the information which we have available to us doubles every five years.

A large New York insurer sends details of medical claims to Caribbean Data Services in the Dominican Republic by plane. Details are entered onto computer and transmitted back to New York by satellite and leased communication lines. The whole process is as quick – and cheaper – than doing it in New York.

(Adapted from John Maxwell Hamilton, *Keeping up with the Information*)

It's not just business that is reaping the benefits. More and more schools are going on-line.

Duncan Nichol, Former Chief Executive of the NHS Executive, quoted in the *IM&T Strategy Overview*, NHS Management Executive, 1992

Information systems can help improve services to meet public need, increase output to match rising expectations and harness the skills of the workforce to greater effect. They can help improve care, increase efficiency and raise effectiveness. Information systems can transform the way the NHS [National Health Service] functions as a family of organisations and professionals committed to improving the health of the nation.

The revolution can be accessible to all:

> The French Minitel system ensures that all homes and businesses have potential access to a massive computer network. Plug a shoe-sized terminal – or indeed your own computer – into the phone socket and you can carry out business, book travel, manage your finance, and share information.

■ The new infrastructure – speed, volume, overload?

The new equation is a direct result of the new information infrastructure. The evolution of mass market, affordable yet incredibly fast computers has coincided with the development of new telecommunications networks to create the new information highway. Anyone with a personal computer, some communications software, a modem, and a telephone socket can now log on and nerd out.

In his invaluable book, *New Work Habits For a Radically Changing World*, Price Pritchett lists the following almost incredible facts:

- since 1985, homes and offices in the UK alone have bought 1,700,000 fax machines;
- there are now 40 million e-mail addresses in the world;
- in the last five years over 12 million computers have been sold in the UK;
- in 1982 no one in the UK had a mobile 'phone;
- there are now well over 4 million of the blighters;
- 800,000 people carry pagers;
- there were 30 million messages left in voice mailboxes in the UK in 1994.

Case proven.

Geoffrey Darnton and Sergio Giacoletto argue that the information revolution needs a new infrastructure in just the same way that the industrial revolution needed the new networks of canal, rail, and eventually road transport. Only when that infrastructure is in place can the full impact of the information age be felt.

And the infrastructure is developing fast. Across the world telecommunication companies are laying networks of optical fiber cables. With the deregulation of the industry, other operators – cable television companies, rail networks, high-speed road operators – can provide competing services. The world is fast becoming wired.

The world is fast becoming wired

And the increasing power and speed of computers appears exponential. As Tom Peters argues, in 1980 computers could make 330,000 calculations a second and could already compute equations that were unfeasible for human brains. In 1995 we are expecting "teraflop" machines operating at one trillion calculations a second.

And it's not just speed, but capability. First and second-generation computers were great for crunching numbers. They were precious little use for anything else, especially if you happened not to hold a doctorate in programming. Now computers are starting to think for themselves. Decision support systems are programmed with knowledge provided by experts in the subject. For example, doctors can question an expert medical system to narrow down the problem and arrive at a suitable diagnosis.

Shoshana Zuboff has coined the term "informate" to stress that computers must do more than automate particular tasks and in the process deskill the people who used to do those tasks. She argues that they must be used to empower people and to develop their skills.

And, of course, the real power of computers continues to grow. Unlike the cost. Each year, the cost of computing power will drop by around 30 per cent.

And just think about the way the size of computers has shrunk. They have gone from warehouse size to fingernail size. The first modern computer, ENIAC, was made in 1944. It weighed more than a small herd of elephants, and could do 5,000 calculations a second. Whereas something called the 486 is built on a tiny piece of silicon the size of a fingernail and does 54 million calculations a second.

Who said big is beautiful?

■ The new globalism – blurring of boundaries and frontiers

> National boundaries are tumbling as knowledge reaches the formerly uninformed citizenry, which is no longer willing to sit idly by and let the government do what's "best" for them.

Mel Phelps, *Upside*, June 1991

One of the key characteristics of information is its ability to filter across boundaries and frontiers. Phelps highlights how national frontiers are little obstacle to information flows. Indeed, in these days when a telephone line can carry most information worth having, there is little a country can do to close its borders – short of cutting off the 'phone network.

The "global flexibility" brought about by the information revolution is having a major impact on organizations:

> It is now possible, indeed imperative, for traditional manufacturing companies to function as if borders did not exist at all. ... Businesses of all kinds have become more adept at using information to knit together workers from vastly different locations and cultures.

John Maxwell Hamilton, *Keeping up with the Information*

The fire department in Malmö, Sweden, reaches its database of street routes by contacting a General Electric computer in Cleveland, Ohio.

The principal dynamic in organizational change in recent years has been the drive to break down borders, to work across boundaries. Organizations that stick rigidly to hierarchical, departmental structures are going to the wall in droves. New organizations with matrix structures, centered around the creation of cross-functional project teams, are the ones that are going places.

Geoffrey
Darnton
and Sergio
Giacoletto,
*Information in
the Enterprise:
It's more than
Technology*

> One of the most important reasons why so many enterprises do not benefit from IT is that they have allowed themselves to be organized along strictly departmental or functional lines. ... Pure top-down, central planning is not effective because of the increasing complexity of the information processing task.

Edward Lawler argues that an organization's information systems must promote the open flow of information. He comments that staff must have information to be able to "direct and manage themselves, operate with reduced hierarchy and be involved in the business."

And, indeed, the interface between organizations is getting fuzzier. The days when firms screwed their suppliers for every last penny are gone as customer–supplier partnerships flourish. Examples such as Marks & Spencer in retailing are many. But partnerships are developing elsewhere – between healthcare organizations within the UK's "health market," between educational organizations and industry; between health, social service, and education professionals in child care.

And information is driving these transformations. It is the realization that they must share information that pushes customers into closer relationships with their suppliers. It is the knowledge of what might happen if they don't share information about child abuse that brings together health, social service, and education professionals.

■ The new paradox – more is less?

The irony is this. With ever mushrooming quantities of information around us, are we any better prepared to take decisions?

Increasingly we hear people saying that despite all the paperwork surrounding them, they need to take decisions with high levels of uncertainty.

It's a problem that has always faced the professions. What marks out a top quality professional is his ability to back up his judgment. Now we are all in the same boat.

Handy has highlighted the growth in uncertainty that we all face as jobs for life and steady careers go out the window. The uncertainty is now all around us. We are faced with some key questions:

- How can we be sure about what is the right information to seek in the first place?

- How can we trust the information we receive sufficiently to base decisions on it?

- How can we be sure that the information we sift out is not in fact vital?

■ The new language – surfing the web?!

Don't believe anyone who tells you that language is neutral. No, it's packed with politics. It is a battleground and they who control the words win the battle. This is probably why Marxists and capitalists and indeed all the other "ists" have been fighting over language for years.

And what have we got in this new information age – well a new language, of course. To many the new language is an abomination. It is crammed with new words, new concepts, and new sentence constructions. It is a credit to the USA, which has a much healthier attitude to language than Britain, for instance, that the new language has been welcomed and explored. There is a joy in coining new words to describe new things. And the language is likely to continue developing. To be in the revolution you need to at least understand what the revolutionaries are saying and, indeed, meaning.

Major changes are accompanied by changes in language. The industrial revolution rewrote the dictionary and the information revolution is doing the same

So to be one of the Trotsky club you had to understand a word like *dialectic*. You wouldn't get far sitting in a slightly smoky revolutionary gathering with a mystified look on your face. To be in the information age gang, it helps at least to know your RAM from your Web. We give you access to some of this new coinage later in the book.

But doubts do remain. Are we being serious?

- Is it really possible to "surf" a "web"?
- Can you really become a "propeller head"?
- Who needs 500K when you can get a megabyte?

Major changes are accompanied by changes in language. The industrial revolution rewrote the dictionary and the information revolution is doing the same.

But don't get too carried away. Surfing the Web isn't really surfing at all. There are actually no fresh waves, sea gulls, ice creams, bikinis, swimming trunks, sun lotion, children playing, or ozone smells. In fact, it just means rather sad people sitting in darkened rooms who have nothing better to do with their time than stare at a computer screen.

The new hunter-gatherers – or the rise of the information champion

The final cornerstone brings us to the title and topic of the book – the information champions who will truly surf the wave of the information age. How will we recognize them?

One thing's for sure. They won't be the technonerds and the propellor heads who zap their way across the Internet in pursuit of Bruce Springsteen messages.

Peter Drucker describes them as "knowledge workers", specialists who are neither "bosses" nor "workers":

> Their own field may be quite narrow. But in it they know more than the boss – and they know it. In their field they are superior to their employer, no matter how low their standing in the organizational hierarchy.

Peter Drucker,
*The New
Realities*

Geoffrey Darnton and Sergio Giacoletto talk about them as information "professionals":

> More and more professionals make decisions based on information they receive directly. Eventually an enterprise will comprise a network of professionals using sophisticated information technology to enhance their own information processing capacity.

Geoffrey
Darnton
and Sergio
Giacoletto,
*Information in
the Enterprise:
It's more than
Technology*

We don't necessarily see the information champion as a specialist – indeed, we believe that, while he may well have important specialist skills, it will be his mastery of some key generic skills that will mark him out. We believe that he does have some characteristics of professionals – but without the obsession with status that has dogged the traditional professionals.

What marks out information champions is a number of key characteristics:

- They **understand**. They understand that knowledge is the key asset of organizations.

- They are not scared of **new technology**. They do not use it for its own sake. They use it when needed and continue to explore the possibilities it offers.

- They will be **learners**. Gone are the days when learning stopped when you left school. Faced with the new equation and the new globalism, information champions will be good at learning and they will learn continually.

It's been estimated that knowledge is doubling about every seven years and that in technical fields, in particular, half of what students learn in their first year of college is obsolete by the time they graduate. This means that continuous learning is absolutely essential in the information age.

- Equally, they will be good at helping others to learn – they will be **coaches**. There success will show, not just in their own ability to adapt to constant change and new challenges, but also in helping others to do the same.

- They will be **leaders** rather than, or as well as, being managers. Their leadership will be founded on their competence and the respect they inspire in those around them, not on the status arising from their place in the hierarchy. And they will be constantly needing to reaffirm their leadership in the face of new challenges.

- They will be effective **members of self-managing teams.** The combination of the new infrastructure with the new paradox means that no one can survive alone for very long in the new information world. Information champions will work best in self-managing teams – teams that may fluctuate in shape, form, and membership according to the circumstances and challenges they face.

- They will be **hunter gatherers of information.** They will know where to look for information, how to obtain it effectively and how to make sense of it when they obtain it.

- Faced by the new paradox, they will be effective **decision makers** in the midst of the avalanche of information and the absence of certainty. It's the quality of decision making that's likely to be the touchstone for success in the new age and decision making comes from good and effective and up-to-date information. That's how people will be judged and it's these new information champions that are likely to be at the forefront of the revolution pushing it forward.

Tomorrow's managers will take it for granted that they can use IT. They'll take for granted that information is their most valuable resource. They'll take for granted that it's their job to use this information in order to be creative and generate new ideas. They'll take for granted that they will need to be constantly reskilling in order to survive.

But for today's managers the challenges are particularly difficult. If they don't really get to grips with it then they're likely to be left behind and there may well be no place for them.

We will return in much greater detail to the skills of information champions – and what you can do to develop them – in later chapters. But before getting too carried away, we will go on to look at the downside of the revolution.

References

Adams, D. "The ways of the world", in *The Guardian*, Monday Oct. 9, 1995.

Darnton, G. and Giacoletto, S. *Information in the Enterprise: It's more than Technology*. Digital Press/Butterworth Heinemann, London, 1992.

Drucker, P. *The New Realities*. Mandarin. London.

Haywood, T. *Info-rich, Info-poor: Access and Exchange in the Global Information Society*. Bowkar-Saur, London, 1995.

Lawler, E. *The Ultimate Advantage: Creating the High Involvement Organisation*. Jossey-Bass, San Fransisco, 1992.

Maxwell Hamilton, J. "Keeping up with the Information" in Moss Kanter R., Stein, B. and Jick, D. *The Challenge of Organisational Change*. Free Press, New York, 1992.

NHS Executive. *IM&T Strategy overview*. NHS Executive, Leeds, 1992.

Peters, T. *Liberation Management*. Pan Books, London, 1992.

Phelps, M. *Upside*, 1991. Quoted in Peters, T. above.

Pritchett, P. *The Employee Handbook of New Work Habits for a Radically Changing World*, Pritchett Associates, 1994.

Steiner, G. *Language and Silence*.

Toffler, A. *Powershift: Knowledge, Wealth and Violence at the Edge of the 21st Century*. Bantam Books, 1990.

Zuboff, S. *In the Age of the Smart Machine*. Heinemann, London, 1988.

chapter two

SOME MIGHTY CHALLENGES IN THE INFORMATION AGE

This chapter looks at some of the challenges we need to acknowledge and tackle if we are to thrive and survive in the new reality that confronts us

"What will you do now that anything is possible?"

Sheridan le Fanu,
*nineteenth
century writer
and visionary*

Changing times: changing minds

Any great change or shift is likely to bring with it huge challenges and this *information age* we are in is no different.

New ages bring new challenges. They tend to turn accepted ideas upside down and raise serious questions about the way we have done things in the past and the way we should do things in the future.

The information age confronts many of our deep held views about the way organizations are, and indeed about the way people behave within them. This chapter looks at some of the challenges we need to acknowledge and tackle if we are to thrive and survive in the new reality that confronts us.

Unquestionably, we will leave behind many of the ways that things have always worked. Organizations will change rapidly and unpredictably.

With revolutions there's little predicting how things will turn out in the end. Sometimes things don't turn out for the best.

I was on a seminar on creativity back in the 1980s. The seminar participants came from universities all around the world. I was in my early twenties and in a moment of youthful vigour said something about "come the revolution, everything will be fine." A little later one of the participants spoke to me. She was from Poland and quietly said that sometimes revolutions are the last thing that anyone wants – after all, look what revolutions had done for Poland.

■ The questions

The new age, like any new age, gets us and the organizations we work in to ask questions, but this time round there are no easy answers.

These are just some of the questions that the new age is likely to ask of us.

- *Information is a unique and vital management resource, but do we really understand it?*
- *Is information a commodity that can be controlled and tied down?*
- *With such an information-rich environment, are we managing it or is it managing us?*
- *Do we need a whole new philosophy in order to survive in this age?*
- *Should we be encouraging information rather than managing it?*
- *How can we turn information into that magical commodity – knowledge and wisdom?*
- *Can businesses get in touch with information and develop a new consciousness to do so?*

And this is just a sample of the questions. But when we stop asking questions then the information age will have passed us by. And in cultures that often value certainty at the expense of doubt, perhaps this is the first major challenge – can we live with change and can we live with uncertainty. And of course can we handle the casualties created by any revolution?

Difficult questions all, and the resulting changes may be messy and possibly costly too.

■ The walking wounded and the dispossessed

The information age is likely to create new classes of haves and have-nots.

Those able to access and use information effectively will rank amongst the haves: the cut-off point for have-nots may be far higher in the pyramid than before. Slip behind as a business and as a manager and a quick dose of radical downsizing or restructuring is likely to see you off.

Where in the industrial revolution, despite a veneer of Victorian concern, the poor found themselves locked away and driven towards forced labour – what will happen to the new information poor? Perhaps they will end up in some dusty data warehouse.

And what will the winners look like? According to *Visions of Life in 2045*, by European IT specialists CMG, a group of technocrats and superworkers will be the real winners in the near future. The superworkers will have electronic devices implanted in their brains, making them part human, part mega database.

Sound farfetched? Maybe, but here's another vision of what the winners will look like – chief learning officers (CLOs). With all this information flying around, organizations are employing people to make sure that the whole business knows how to learn. US West has created just such a post. The holder spends time riding around Arizona with repairmen and found that his performance improved with regular feedback from supervisors. Simple stuff, but the lesson applied to the company's 53,000 employees could have some impact. And the problem as the CLO, Richard Baumbush, points out was that: "As a company we were not capturing knowledge."

As companies become more and more far-flung and connected by 'phone lines and the like, the challenge is for the company to keep learning and using information to generate real knowledge. So expect more posts like chief knowledge officer and director of knowledge management and creativity director, and the like. These are likely to be the winners in the information age and for a CLO there may not be a computer in sight – just people and a company that need to keep learning in order to survive.

And the losers? What about the great legions of the middle class and traditional professions? The middle class in most parts of the world has always been concerned with slipping through the net. Entering the professions has been seen as a protection against this prospect. Education and professional status have been seen as portable and enduring. But what happens as even the professions are confronted with the need to learn new information skills? Will the net hold out?

Other losers: people who can't switch on a computer. People who think they've learned all they need to. People who think they've got their qualifications so why learn more. People who know everything by experience, and so don't need to keep abreast of all the information tumbling in.

And there is a danger that many of the losers may be older people. It is true that youngsters often are very comfortable with computers and the language of the information age. Research has backed this up. The risk is that organizations will get younger and younger in terms of staff profile. Older people will be forced out if it is thought that they do not have computer and information age know-how.

On the one hand, there are advantages to this. You get a young, dynamic, possibly manic organization. But an all-young company may lack wisdom, judgment, and experience in vital areas. Socially it may become an unpleasant bear pit. Companies need older people who have a life outside work – people with children, interests, and passions outside the workplace, people who can keep a cool head, people who know there is more to life than work. A balanced age, class, and gender profile is essential for balanced diverse organizations. If the old don't adapt or are pushed out unfairly we may create organizations that are just no damn fun to work in.

So what are the challenges and how will we hold up in the face of them?

1 Control as a thing of the past

Old dynasties, new world

Back in the 1980s, the USSR counterrevolution was in the air. The old communist military decided that Boris Yeltsin was threatening to change things too much and too quickly, and, therefore, decided to reassert control.

What they hadn't banked on was the new power of information, and the fact that it's simply resistant to control in the old ways. Information is no longer the simple slave of the dominant regime.

Like countless dictatorships before, the military tried the old ways. It took over the television station and the newspapers. It played official music over the news station. It put troops on the streets. The media was targeted and information was meant to be closely controlled. In the past, bringing the blanket down in this way had worked just fine.

But the military hadn't counted on the uncontrollable nature of information today.

So Yeltsin holed up in an office with telephones and fax machines. He kept up a steady stream of alternative information to the regions and to his supporters and to the world's press using those fax machines.

What's more, satellite television had made wide scale inroads into the communist bloc. The old guard may have been able to stop state television but the people of the Soviet Union were able to tune into CNN and other international broadcasts, to find out exactly what was happening.

The military couldn't quiet things down however hard they tried. So Yeltsin, armed with a loaded kalashnikov, fueled by strong vodka, and aided by a new information infrastructure, defeated the old guard.

This dealt a severe blow to political ideology and the old ways of looking at information and made a clear statement: These days you simply can't put the lid on a story.

Information is now widely available. Control is well nigh impossible, and it's the same issue that organizations, big and small, have been wrestling with.

The question is what do you do when the old ways of controlling information simply won't do? You can't just send in the troops.

In the 1970s dissidents plastered China's Democracy Wall with criticism of the regime. The regime then spent a month removing the posters and arrested the ringleaders. Information controlled.

Today, China is waging a futile battle against cyberspace. Beijing has banned new memberships of the Internet. Existing members must register with the police. But to no avail. A vast underground network of users is beginning to grow – and with a population of 1.2 billion, the tide will be impossible to stem.

■ Information as creative energy

Commentators have pointed out that information is a new creative energy of the universe.

Our problem is that we've looked at information as something which is there for us to control. It is simply a means to an end.

This old way of looking at things meant that information was seen as a commodity - something we simply transfer from one place to another – and once that is done, its use is past.

Of course, this rather classical view of information also meant that we were the ones that controlled it.

The problem is though that with the growth and the amount of information available and the speed with which it can be transmitted, this will no longer do.

Where in the past we expected to manage information, we now need to see it in a different kind of way. Information becomes a more organic, living entity, one that we plug into and enjoy, rather than simply control.

And it's here that we find one of the first main dilemmas faced by modern organizations and modern people in them.

The great fear is that information will run wild, out-of-control. The response sometimes is to put a rigid control in place.

> Up to now we've put a kind of organizational chastity belt on information, seeing this as a management control. What's become clear is that it's simply uncontrollable

In other words, up to now we've put a kind of organizational chastity belt on information, seeing this as a management control. What's become clear is that it's simply uncontrollable. It is running loose in our organizations, unfettered and uncontrolled, doing as it will.

■ Finding alternatives

The one option is to behave rather like the communist old guard: send the troops out onto the streets, regain control of media and keep information centralized, nailed down, and a privilege. But this is just as likely to fail in organizations as it did on the streets of Russia.

We are in an information-rich environment and an environment that is likely to get even richer.

So what's the alternative?

Well, if we don't see information as something to be controlled, maybe we should start to see it as more vital, freer, and liberating.

This clearly is a challenge and it's an issue which organizations are going to have to wrestle with and come to terms with over the years. Especially as controlling information has often been a way of guarding power in organizations.

Information out of control

In *Managing out of bounds*, Gary Hamell, a visiting professor of strategic and international management at London Business School, sets out a vision of a world in which information is out of control, and in which organizations need to come to terms with this.

For Hamell, we've left the Machine Age behind and are now moving inexorably to the Information Age. For him, this will challenge all our practices of management and our view of what organizations actually are.

In particular, it would mean that where traditionally authority was vested top down, and information guarded, hoarded, and given only on a need-to-know basis, today the spread of information and the ease with which it can be obtained will make for a much more democratic, if not anarchic, organization.

Personal computers and corporate e-mail systems are just two of the things which are making organizations much more of an information democracy, and with democracy, the old lines of authority no longer work.

Organizations are increasingly finding that e-mail is being used as a kind of jungle telegraph sending around information and misinformation in a quite uncontrolled way.

Where the temptation is to simply put the lid on this, the difficulty organizations face is that it's uncontrollable.

What's more, as organizations increasingly spread out with people working from home, the boundaries of control are likely to shift and in many cases disintegrate. Where in the old days you could pop down and see staff, they now may well be on the end of a telephone many miles away. The growth of virtual working and distance working have made the lines of control even more difficult to enforce.

As the geographic boundaries break down and the information boundaries change, firms are no longer able to exert such tight control. This brings about important questions that will need to be resolved about empowerment, distance, and the like.

Everything is changing and boundaries are gone – you can even get married over the Internet.

2 Is there value in the information age?

But when the boundaries are gone and when democracy strikes what happens about the certainties we're used to? What do we do when anything is possible?

Here a very interesting debate is developing about some of the real dangers that we face.

In the UK, the former Archbishop of York, Lord Habgood, has attacked the information age in a speech on BBC Radio 4. It's all too easy to write off senior churchmen as voices from the past, but Habgood raises some crucial and very important points about the information age. His plea in short is: *"Where is the value in this information age?"*

For Habgood, the increase in democratization and the availability of information is leading to a rather dangerous relativism. As he puts it:

"Knowledge is just an endless succession of human opinions and there are no abiding truths or principles."

For Habgood, the surfer on the Internet is simply isolating himself from the world, and, more than this, he's not able to attach value to different kinds of information. As such one is merely moving from one simple gratification to another without applying, thinking through, or understanding what the information means.

On the internet, one can surf quickly between popular TV sitcoms to gossip, to a report on the war in Bosnia, or other international hot spots.

For Lord Habgood, the problem is that there's no sense of value here. As he says:

"To have almost limitless power to call up any image to convey and receive information without any restraints, to create, as it were, one's own world could reinforce the dangerous perception that life has no purpose beyond individual self-gratification."

Essentially what Habgood is talking about, and what other commentators have pointed out too, is the fact that all this information may not lead to wisdom. This leads to a kind of shopping cart approach to life where people pull information off the shelf, look at it and cast it away, and then pull off more information.

> **The big challenge we face in the information age is learning from it, gaining wisdom from all this information. And the cautionary note sounded is a valuable one.**

We wait to find out whether this information will actually be turned into anything useful or whether it will simply be just another example of the world speeding up, of images taking the place of meaning.

Ask yourself if we any wiser now than we were:

- 50 years ago,

- 100 years ago,

- 150 years ago.

3 The wrong people for the job

■ Technofiles, technophobes, and propeller heads

Another major issue is simply whether the people who are in authority are really cut out to deal with a new age. And whether the new breed of people with information knowledge is capable of leading us to a new understanding of what is possible. Put simply, it looks very much as though the wrong people may be in the wrong job. It also looks as if the rise of computer nerdism may scupper the move to the new.

This is probably one of the features of revolutions – that those already in power get swept away by the revolution and only the canny, the corrupt, the dubious or the Machiavellian seem able to survive.

The Henley Centre, the UK forecasting group, in a survey published on March 30, 1995 identified four distinctive user groups for information technology:

- **Technofiles.** These are estimated as 24 percent of the population. Technofiles are enthusiastic about technology in a general sense and also show a high level of interest in the applications of new technology. They are concentrated among the under 35s, are more likely to be male than female, and are more likely to belong to social grades C1 and AB.

- **Aspirational technofiles.** These are estimated to represent 22 percent of the population. They are excited in the general sense about technology but are much less interested in its applications. They are more likely to be male than female and are more concentrated in the AB social grade.

- **Functionals.** These are estimated as 25 percent of the population. They claim to be uninterested in technology, but are not actually hostile to its applications, especially in those areas which offer an enhancement of existing services. These consumers are more likely to be male than female and are more numerous among the over 45s.

- **Technophobes.** These are estimated to make up 28 percent of the population. They are hostile to technology at all levels and are skeptical about whether technology can offer anything new. Technophobes are concentrated in the over 60 age group, are more likely to be female than male, and are fairly evenly distributed throughout the social grades.

In this disturbing piece of research, almost 30 percent of people in the UK alone were said to be technophobes, and the pattern is likely to be repeated elsewhere in the world. In other words, there are people actively hostile to technology at all levels and skeptical about whether it can offer anything new. This group is likely to be older with the majority of people being in the over 60 age group, although not exclusively so. Technophobes are distributed amongst all social grades. It begs a worrying question. How do organizations embrace a new age if those at the helm are looking in the wrong direction?

> **How do organizations embrace a new age if those at the helm are looking in the wrong direction?**

The message here is clear – the information revolution may well be blocked if people of power and influence in organizations are against it. In many ways, the information revolution is caught between the devil and the deep blue sea.

On the one hand, there are the technophobes, often perching midway or toward the tip of organizations, but equally there is the problem of "propeller heads" or technobores.

A propeller head is basically someone who is so far gone in his love of technology that he is unable to speak a sensible version of the language anymore. Nor can he see the world as it is, rather than as he would like it to be. This is how one person described a propeller head to us:

> "It's really amazing when you actually get to talk to these propeller heads. Their mouths are opening and sounds are coming out, but they actually aren't saying anything that even relatively sophisticated people in terms of IT could understand."

Peter Robinson,
AFC Computers

It's quite scary to think that these are normal people, who were actually humans at one stage before this obsession took over. It's a rather frivolous observation, but it's probably easy enough to spot one of these propeller heads.

The nasty haircut, the flared trousers, the disk tucked in the top pocket and the duffel coats are a give away, but not the only give away. Sometimes propeller heads actually take on human guise and can gain a good deal of power and influence.

Enough of the jokes, because there is a real issue here. The ownership of the new technology has been vested in IT people. This has contributed to the fact that the benefits of the information age have not been communicated to people. The systems the IT people have invented work technically but have not taken enough account of the fact that many people are at a stage in life where learning about computers is a big deal.

The company you keep

Maybe you judge a revolution by the people involved. In this case the company kept by the information age is, to say the least, questionable. Computer bores and propellor heads are already quite enough, but there is also another strand – the acid computer head.

Timothy Leary, doyen of the 1960s drug culture, latched onto the information age before his death. He saw it as a gateway to the future and was excited by the possibilities it offered. He devoted his last days to making CD ROMS and virtual libraries. He had a Web site. His house became home to various young computer waifs and strays.

He even adapted his famous phrase

Turn on, tune in, drop out.

Before his death it became:

Turn on, tune in, boot up.

4 The volume of information

Clearly another major issue is the sheer volume of information that organizations and managers within them are now exposed to.

> The weekday edition of the *New York Times* contains more information than the average person was likely to come across during a lifetime in seventeenth century England.

Wright, Hodgson, and Craner in **The Future of Leadership** point out that:

> Executives find themselves in a wind tunnel with sheaves of paper being propelled towards them. They catch one and rush around pretending they know the answer. All they've found is part of the jigsaw.

Wright, Hodgson, and Craner, *The Future of Leadership*

In other words, the sheer volume of information makes certainty much more difficult and indeed makes it far more difficult to function day to day.

Organizations become almost addicted to information. In many organizations there are monthly progress checks, quarterly reports, evaluations, and so forth. And the question is continually and rather nervously expressed, how can we trust the information we're getting, how can we handle it all, how can we make an intelligent decision with so much information available?

Put simply, there is an overload of information out there and it's speedily swamping even the more enterprising and modern manager and organization. *Information rich can mean information overloaded.*

The key is being able to turn that information into useful knowledge and indeed, more broadly, into some kind of wisdom, but how to do it in the middle of an avalanche is a more than difficult question.

It's one of those key challenges that the information age presents and one that this book hopes, in part, to help answer.

5 Increasing distances

Distance is one of the real challenges the information age presents. In many ways, looking back at the old days things seem deceptively simple. People went to work and came home again in the evening. These days, with the advanced growth of telecoms, the world is a far smaller place – people are not tied to the workplace. Two of the authors writing this book work from home and the dismal days of commuting, offices and office politics are dim and distant memories. What has made this change possible is telecommunications.

Real ideas are often generated by people in the same room talking to each other, interacting, arguing, resolving, and coming up with that magic alchemy that creates progress and negotiation, and indeed ideas.

People are increasingly able to work at a distance from their workplace. It's estimated that even at this precise moment, 270 million people in the US spend at least 20 per cent of their working week away from the office, connected up to telecommunications.

Now clearly, working at a distance can be effective, but it surely creates challenges too. There are historical, social, and psychological reasons why humans have joined up to work together in organizations. They like the companionship. If you sit next to someone communication problems are eased. It often feels good to be part of an environment and team. The social aspect leads to team spirit and bonding and adds value to lives outside work and in.

Experience shows that organizations and the people working for them can become sterile and overly task focussed when working at a distance.

Real ideas are often generated by people in the same room talking to each other, interacting, arguing, resolving, and coming up with that magic alchemy that creates progress and negotiation, and indeed ideas.

Research in the late 1970s by Tom Allen at the Massachusetts Institute of Technology found that collaboration between specialists improved with close physical proximity. They found that just a few floors separating people led to collaboration suffering considerably. So how on earth can we square this with the growth of people beginning to work from home and companies spread to the four winds? Surely the more diverse organizations become, the more communication problems there will be – regardless of modems and the like.

We have seen that many companies have reacted against these wide distances that have crept into organizations.

> In 1994, Texas Instruments put the brake on its global development network and relocated engineers to fewer sites. In short, it started to move the organization back toward the center rather than relying on global telecommunications.
>
> Ford has done very much the same, moving 500 designers, engineers, and managers to just one location, working cheek by jowl, generating ideas in the old fashioned way.

It's rather ironic that, despite these new technological advances in communications, being able to communicate with people at the touch of a button, there's no substitute for actually being close.

There's certainly been a clash between co-location and virtual location. But the truth is that the two can go hand in hand.

Ford may have rammed people together but it also upped the electronic communications. In 12 months it doubled the amount of transatlantic video conferencing to support the new organization. Ford executives will still tell you that quality face-to-face communication is better than the electronic equivalent, but you can't run a modern organization without electronic communication too. And there's nothing to replace the unique benefits of getting people into a room for one week and asking them to thrash out a problem.

The key point is that electronic communications are good at transferring data and processing information. They are not so good at creating new concepts and knowledge. So no amount of virtuality can really substitute for the magic of sitting around and creating ideas out of nothing.

6 Incredible shrinking personal space

Another simple problem with the information age is the way that it bears down on people and reduces the divide between home and work.

Once upon a time you came home and left the office behind. These days that's not so easy. You're likely to have at the very least an answerphone and possibly a fax machine at home. Many modern homes closely resemble the modern office with modems, computers, and even video conferencing.

British management guru John Harvey-Jones talks from the heart when he bemoans the loss of personal space that follows from the move to working from home. And with modern telecommunications his plight is likely to be repeated by others maybe millions of times.

John Harvey-Jones,
Managing to Survive

> I have discovered for myself that working from home means the loss of one's private space and time to a much greater degree than I had envisaged. The fact that your work is in your home rapidly erodes the difference between leisure time and work. Moreover, even though it is perfectly easy to keep in contact with other people through the telephone and the fax machine, these contacts are almost bound to be much more closely related to the perceived immediate issues than the general gossip and chat which happens when you meet people face to face.

Harvey-Jones goes on to point out the danger here.

> The contribution which the human mind makes to work and business is very much one of picking up information from tiny, seemingly insignificant trifles and relating them to new ideas and concepts.

Harvey-Jones paints a rather bleak picture and ends by saying that the new ways of working brought about as a result of the information age have led to his most cherished thing – home life – suffering profoundly. And if John Harvey-Jones suffers, then there is a warning here for everyone.

This closing down of personal space has really started to put the pressure on employees and the cracks are beginning to show. Nearly half the respondents to a recent survey reported that their companies interrupted holidays and sickness absence with questions related to work. And it's new technology that carries much of the blame.

Lucy Calloway wrote in the *Financial Times*:

> Thanks to the fax and the mobile 'phone, no-one is ever out of touch, even if they take their holidays on the top of a mountain.

Lucy Calloway,
Financial Times

You can add to this laptops and e-mail which can both climb mountains too. This leads onto another problem that seems to be around at the moment in terms of personal space. Information overload through e-mail.

Tim Jackson states in the *Financial Times* that:

> Many people inside US companies receive over 100 e-mail messages a day, many superfluous. This can cause enormous stress.

When you think that in the US job stress has been estimated to cost industry around $140 billion a year, while in the UK, inefficiencies arising from stress have been estimated as costing up to 10 per cent of the gross national product, you really have a problem. And e-mail does seem to be making life a lot more difficult.

There's no substitute for teams and there's no substitute for people working together. These are the things that make people feel valued at work and cut out that all important stress, and as e-mail becomes more and more intrusive in people's daily lives, what is that likely to mean for people?

■ Danger e-mail

Indeed e-mail can cause a number of problems. For a start, it's IT centered rather than people centered. This can make it particularly unappealing. More than anything else, it adds to a kind of overburdening of people's work days. Too many messages are sent to too many people with too little time.

It just adds to this feeling of information overload and worryingly e-mail can lead to cliques and counter-information networks as we've seen before. This can prove to be a real problem for organizations to manage.

We've come across one example where a secretary mounted a campaign of abuse against a colleague, sending regular e-mail bulletins to other members of staff criticizing her appearance and behavior. Managers (and the woman targeted by the campaign) were unaware of what was happening – but all too aware that the group simply didn't work efficiently as a team. It was only when a systems problem arose that the management's attention was drawn to these unexpected and highly abusive files. The perpetrator was severely disciplined.

What this means is that people do need to have e-mail etiquette training, that is training as to when and where to use e-mail, rather than just how to use it.

E-mail is also there to be listened to as well as just keeping information down. And some organizations may need to consider capping or limiting the use of the Internet and e-mail just to free up some time and space.

In a recent review of how top managers are using IT now, one respondent explained a rather worrying use of e-mail:

"Sometimes it's difficult to ask somebody to come up into your office and tell him you screwed up. So I use e-mail as a face-saving device. I can say things on e-mail that I wouldn't say face-to-face. I use e-mail to scream at someone. You can go and scream a message across and people can read it privately. Then we sort it out later face-to-face."

The idea of managers persecuting staff through such methods and avoiding face-to-face contact is really quite scary. It isn't just the person himself using e-mail as a substitute, it's also the problem of how much time people have taken up using it.

Computer Associates, the world's biggest software company, has decided that e-mail is stopping people from getting on with their work. It felt that too many people were being interrupted by the large number of messages that appeared on their screens all day says J. Hough, Marketing Director of CA in the UK. So the company now limits its e-mail service to certain times of the day, around 10.00am to lunchtime. Outside these message periods employees can compose messages but they can't actually send them. So e-mail can be misused and one of the problems is that people find e-mail just too easy to send. It requires far less effort than picking up the 'phone and certainly much less effort than going and mailing a letter.

> **The truth is though that there are some pretty serious civil liberties issues raised by this new information age.**

7 How to keep information private

This leads to one of the key issues that the new information revolution and the information age presents to us. How private is information? How secure? How safe is it? It's interesting that much of the American literature on the information age has had a marked conspiracy theory ring to it – watch out, big brother is watching you. This is probably because the Internet was developed by the American military and that many info heads in the US writing fraternity took too many drugs in the 1960s.

The truth is though that there are some pretty serious civil liberties issues raised by this new information age.

Vast powerful databases can hold a variety of very personal data about people. Because the Internet itself contains just a few points that most users pass through, there's a potential for massive data collection and this in turn may lead to people selling on data and the development of large catalogs. And it's the people who own the access to and the creation of information who have real power.

Newer networks allow people to research complex social problems, but the scope for abuse is just as great here. Already there are plans to use the technology to identify children as young as six who have the potential to be criminals. Newer networks can use unique files from individuals and this will allow them to just simply go and find out all the information available on someone at a certain address.

Currently in the UK, much of this rather sensitive information is on government databases, each stored on the national record system. But the chances are that this may get into the wrong hands, and, in the future, there may be some powerful and difficult decisions to take about civil liberties. Even if we ignore this, the truth is that more and more information is stored about people.

Also in the offing is a possible unified database which would be a living encyclopaedia incorporating all existing databases. It may not seem a bad thing for people to be able to find out how many children you have, their ages, your marital status, but if the details get more personal, it could be rather worrying.

A recent court case in the United States highlighted how out of hand things can get. A man brought a civil action after repeatedly failing to gain approval for insurance policies, bank loans, and credit card applications. After two years, in exasperation, he decided to find out why. The cause was a clerical error – an application had been incorrectly entered into the computer. It stated he had taken an AIDs test.

8 How to keep information secure

Another issue thrown up by this new age we live in is the question of security. The Internet is a notoriously insecure environment, though it is true that new inscription methods have been designed to counter this.

Visa and Eurocard, for instance, have just launched a new inscription drive that will mean that shopping on the Internet is actually more secure. However, the growing instances of hacking and data fraud emphasize that companies can no longer rely solely on staff-based security systems – and that's why automatic security systems are increasingly needed.

> Studies in the USA and Britain have shown that Internet users are at risk from on-line communication. There is even a syndrome to describe this – Internet Addiction Syndrome

Whatever system a company uses, the issue of data security is becoming more and more important.

9 How to remain "dependence free"

There is a growing body of evidence that shows that the tools of the computer age – like the Internet – can be highly addictive.

Studies in the USA and Britain have shown that Internet users are at risk from on-line communication. There is even a syndrome to describe this – Internet Addiction Syndrome (IAD). Here is a list of the symptoms, so you can check to see whether you are a victim.

The telltale symptoms of IAD are:

- Loss of control over how long you spend on the Internet,
- Lying to your spouse about how long you spend on-line,
- Logging on the moment you wake up in the morning,
- Needing to spend longer and longer on-line to get satisfaction,

- Recurring dreams and fantasies about what is happening on the Internet,

- Repeated and unsuccessful attempts to cut down the time you spend on-line.

> Kimberly Young, professor of psychology at Pittsburgh University, claims that lives are being ruined and that the Intenet addiction can be every bit as powerful as that for alcohol and drugs. Typically, it strikes younger people, and especially those who have never used a PC before connecting to the Internet.

Interestingly, the problem does not seem to strike sad people who previously had unsatisfactory lives. It affects people who simply find the virtual world so compelling that "real" life no longer matches up to it. People get a high. There are now support groups to help people come off the Internet drug.

And it isn't just dependence on the Internet that is a problem. The long-term effects of using new technology have not as yet been measured. There are likely to be new illnesses and consequences. We already have a batch of people struck down by RSI (repetitive strain injury) from using keyboards.

In the world of the information age there are now the first moves to establish common standards on the Internet.

There is a scare that mobile 'phones may lead to cancer. As someone said, the Internet is simply the first path cut through the jungle of cyberspace. Who knows what terrors await us in that dark and unknown jungle?

10 How to establish common standards

In Britain when the railways were first built there was no standard gauge for the different track sections of the network. This led to problems as trains from one company could only operate on its own company track. This was resolved by establishing a standard gauge.

In the world of the information age there are now the first moves to establish common standards on the Internet. But it is still very early days and the challenge remains as to whether standards can be established without curbing the creativity inherent in the system.

11 How to keep visual personalities intact

And finally, a big issue confronting organizations is how to keep their visual personalities intact.

Organizations spend millions of pounds establishing a brand image. This means consistently promoting the same image to customers. The information age and the freedom it offers has put this under threat.

With DTP and other graphics packages any Tom, Dick, or Harry can play the designer. This means that where the visual identity was once controlled and consistent, it can now be chipped away by amateur designers doing their own thing. Before you know it, posters and newsletters can be coming from every pore.

Also, as companies get into new media, like CD ROM and Web sites, the long-established visual personality can start to break down.

New design guidelines need to be established to control this and make sure that the array of choices does not create design anarchy.

Enthusiasm needs to be harnessed and guidelines established. Brand identities are being lost in the new technological age. Just look at the Internet and you'll see the same Netscape browser atop some of the best household names. Think about it. It's like going into Main Street and seeing above a store's name plate a standard heading set up by the people who built the premises.

The big picture

So the new information age is one of enormous potential and opportunity. It's one in which anything is possible and certainly it will change how we look at the way we communicate.

Clearly the issue of value, wisdom, and learning is important. If there is an overload of information, how does the difficult business of learning become any easier? We'll look at this later on, but it really is a key issue.

The issue of control, that's important too. If boundaries break down in the blink of an eye, a message can be sent to another part of the world, a whole file is transferred.

How do organizations keep control? Or are these really crazy times as Tom Peters assures us they are. In which case, how will organizations control information? What will organizations do when their best laid plans and efforts are undermined, perhaps by rogue appearances of information on the Internet, or indeed by e-mail? What will organizations do when they can no longer guarantee that their information is secure? And what will organizations do when employees' personal space is increasingly hemmed in by the sheer availability of information, and the way people can keep in touch so easily? It's a double-edged sword.

It certainly isn't a panacea for organizational or human happiness, but what it means is that change is likely to become institutionalized.

■ A final word

We all love the possibilities the new age offers, but do keep a handle on reality.

Remember that many great ideas never actually make it. In 1874 H. Bessember came up with a surefire idea – the self-leveling ship saloon. It was the ideal cure for sea sickness. The idea was that it kept the passengers level while the ship rolled. It was, in fact, a disaster. On the first voyage involving the invention, the saloon veered dangerously from side to side. Moving from the self-leveling saloon to the rest of the ship was like leaping from a moving elevator.

Sea-sickness pills proved to be a better cure for sea sickness.

So amid all the bravado of the information age, and the frankly inflated claims of writers and salesfolk, just remember that one thing is certain – *it sure won't work out like we think.*

But don't get too hung up by reality either because the future and its possibilities beckon. And what looks like magic is, in fact, coming your way now and soon.

You think that there is too much information around. You think that picking 25 choices on the Internet could drive you insane because so much of the information you get back is useless. Well intelligent search engines are on the way. These intelligent agents are search programs that learn about you and tailor searches according to your needs. They will take the dirty work out of searching. They will be your little electronic friends and researchers on the superhighway.

So let's think positive and move on.

References

Tom Allen at the Massachusetts Institute of Technology.
Visions of Life in 2045, CMG, London 1996.

Lucy Calloway in the *Financial Times*, 1996.

Gary Hamell, *Managing out of bounds*.

Lord Habgood, in a speech on BBC Radio 4.

John Harvey-Jones, *Managing to Survive*, Mandarin Books, London, 1993.

Tim Jackson in the *Financial Times*, 1996.

Wright, Hodgson and Craner, *The Future of Leadership*, Pitman, 1996.

"How IT is changing the way you manage," in *World's Executive Digest Technology*, September 1995.

Kimberly Young, professor of psychology at Pittsburgh University.

chapter
three

MODELS FOR THE INFORMATION AGE

A range of models has been
produced, and in this chapter
we aim to give a brief summary
of some of them

Models in the sand

Information management as an intellectual concern has blossomed in recent years. The growing awareness of information as a key resource, coupled with the rapid developments of information technology and telecommunications, have set writers seeking to understand and explain how organizations deal with information. A range of models has been produced, and in this chapter we aim to give a brief summary of some of them.

As with all models, they are but approximations. And given the nature of information – possibly the least tangible of all resources – these models are especially impressionistic. And, in addition – as we mentioned in chapter one – the speed of change is so great that any model runs the risk of being out of date before it is published.

However, they do provide some interesting insights. And they are useful. They are useful because we do need some ways of seeing information that will allow us to view the bigger picture.

The models we explore in this chapter are those of:

- Max Boisot, who brings some of the concepts of cultural anthropology to bear on information management;
- Justin Keen, who takes a somewhat different look at how organizations deal with information;
- The "open systems" approach, which focuses on how information enters, moves around, and leaves an organization;
- Ideas about how "data" may be transformed into information and knowledge;
- Ideas about how information is sent and received;
- The concept of a "virtual marketspace;"
- The concept of data warehousing.

Max Boisot – cultural anthropology

Max Boisot, in his book *Information and Organizations*, argues that information must be seen within the wider context of organizational culture. He defines culture as "involving the structuring and sharing of information within a given social grouping." He argues that each organization will have characteristic behaviors, ideas, and values which are derived from past actions and help to determine future actions.

Boisot's model is based around what he calls the "C-Space" where "C" stands for culture. For Boisot, the essential attributes of information are the extent to which it is:

- **Codified** – highly codified information is understandable only for those who know the code. Examples might be the theorems of quantum physics, or within organizations the monthly accounts summary. At the other extreme, the information in tabloid newspapers is extremely accessible and relatively uncodified.
- **Diffused** – widely diffused information is publicly available. Anyone can get hold of it. At the other extreme is the undiffused information that very few people know exist.

Information within the "C-Space" is defined by the extent to which it is codified and diffused. Boisot argues, for example, that we can define the culture of any organization within the "C-Space" as shown below:

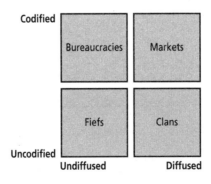

In Boisot's model, for example, bureaucracies tend to use information that is not understandable to the outside world – which may be just as well because they do not intend it to be shared any wider than they can afford.

Boisot's model is interesting in several ways. It can provide a tool for analyzing how your organization tends to treat information – does it hoard it away either by using highly inaccessible, technical language, or by simply making sure no one ever sees the information in the first place? Or does it make free with information, working on the principle that sharing is the first step toward success?

What is more, Boisot's model can help us reflect more profoundly on the information itself. What kind of information is really valuable to the organization? Is it organized and presented in an appropriate manner? Or is it hiding behind professional jargon?

What is interesting, is that as the information age gathers pace, organizations are increasingly likely to group around the diffused end of the box. As we have seen, information is becoming almost impossible to keep to yourself. Organizations will probably spread information more widely.

However, we may find that it becomes more codified than ever because of new jargon and the discourse that is being developed as the information age gathers pace.

It is easy to believe that a person from Mark Twain's day hearing people within an organization discussing issues about information would be likely to think they were speaking a foreign language.

An alternative model of information cultures

Justin Keen (1994) puts forward a slightly different model which reflects not just how organizations treat information , but also the extent to which they seek to manage it and the style they adopt in doing so. He argues that organizations are likely to treat information in one of five ways, as shown in the table below.

Model	Characteristics
Technocratic utopianism	A heavily technical approach to information management, stressing categorization and modeling of an organization's full information assets, with heavy reliance on emerging technologies
Anarchy	No overall information policy, leaving individuals to obtain and manage their own information
Feudalism	Information is managed by individual functions or departments, which define their own information needs and report only limited information to the center
Dictatorship	The board defines information categories and reporting structures, and may not willingly share information with the wider organization
Federalism	Information management is based on consensus and negotiation about information flows

As with all cultural models, it's likely that the overall organization is characterized by a dominant culture, be it federalism, anarchy, or dictatorship. This overall culture will owe much to the style of the senior management team and the way in which information technology is used and managed.

Within this, there are likely to be many subcultures – individual departments or teams which have their own unique style. So while the overall organization may be driving toward technocratic utopianism with large budget mainframe solutions, there may be anarchy in individual sections where enthusiasts are getting personal computers to do what they want, rather than relying on the dinosaur at the center.

We touched on this in chapter two when we saw the difficulty of keeping an organization's visual personality intact.

This way of categorizing information is useful because it high-lights a major problem which organizations face – managing chaos. In an information-rich environment it is perhaps tempting to reach for the technocratic utopian approach. It at least provides comfort that information can be managed. But, again, as we saw in chapter two, the very notion of managing information may be misplaced. Maybe, information should manage us and we simply should opt for a pleasing anarchy and enjoy the ride.

> The systems approach borrows much from the world of biology, where individual organisms, and indeed whole habitats, are seen as systems living in and responding to an environment.

Certainly feudalism and dictatorship do not seem to be adequate approaches faced with the information deluge that there is and the amazing opportunities that there are for using information constructively.

The open systems approach

An alternative way of looking at information in organizations – and one which has a great attraction for many in the field of information management – is the "open systems" approach.

The systems approach borrows much from the world of biology, where individual organisms, and indeed whole habitats, are seen as systems living in and responding to an environment. If the temperature cools, the organism must make an adjustment – whether by hibernating, increasing body temperature, or putting on a sweatshirt. When things warm up, the opposite occurs.

The diagram on the next page shows the organization as an open system. It brings out a number of key points:

● The system operates within a wider environment – hence the word "open" rather than a "closed" system.

- The wider environment places demands on the organization. Demands will come from customers, competitors, changing technologies, new legislation, social trends, and so forth.

- Within the overall organizational system there are several smaller subsystems. Anything in the wider environment which affects the organization will affect each of the subsystems, and they will in turn influence each other.

- The organization must respond to the demands placed upon it. In this process all the parts of the organization in turn affect each other, and the organization influences the wider environment.

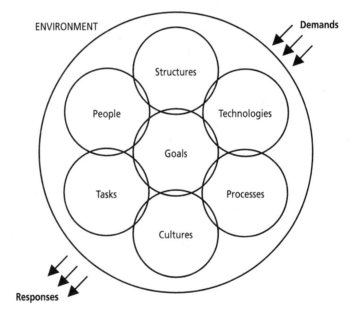

The organization as an open system
(from *Managing Change* by Annabel Broome)

The systems approach offers a different perspective from that of the cultural analysts. It suggests that organizations cannot see themselves as closed entities, hiding away from the wider world amid their jealously guarded secrets. It suggests that they must take account of the wider environment.

Most interestingly, the systems approach may suggest that the more adaptive systems may be those best placed to survive. Just as successful living organisms are those that can respond to changes in the environment, so successful organizations are those that monitor the world beyond their doors and seek to do something about it. Such an analogy supports those – like Rosabeth Moss Kanter – who believe that the most successful organizations are those that are flexible enough to change and grow.

Kodak

One of Moss Kanter's examples of "giants learning to dance" is Kodak. Kodak – saddled with a reputation for avoiding change and facing an increase in competition and loss of market share – sought to emulate the behavior of smaller companies who respond more flexibly to changes in the environment.

Kodak restructured from a highly centralized bureaucracy to a decentralized divisional organization. Decision making was devolved to individual managers. "Horizontal thinking" was encouraged, with people working more closely with their peers in other parts of the organization. Quality and sensitivity to customer needs was placed at the forefront.

From data to information to knowledge

Information is data arranged in a meaningful way for some perceived purpose.

Another model involves looking at ways of changing data first to information and then to knowledge.

Many writers on the subject of information have sought to explain the way that information changes as it is handled by people within organizations. In particular, they have sought to distinguish information from "data" and "knowledge."

Jonathon Liebenau and James Backhouse, *Understanding Information*

For example, Stan Davies and Jim Botkins, writing in the *Harvard Business Review*, foresee a move from simple data to knowledge. For the authors, it's the change in technology that's driving the next wave of economic growth.

The importance of data as an economic factor first became obvious in the 1950s and 1960s. But in those days it took the computer the size of a whole room to collect and sort and store vast amounts of information. This was then programmed by users to produce usable information. Very many people saw themselves in the data collection business. Data and indeed information simply supported the real work of the business – which was to make things or deliver a service or whatever.

More recently computers and standard software have meant that the processes have become far more sophisticated and useful.

It's very possible these days that the information the business produces is often more valuable than the business itself.

What often happens is that the information that the business generates has become the real work of the company. It's the information itself that has gone from being a simple slave of the business to being part of the core business itself.

For Botkin and Davies, the next stage is likely to be when knowledge itself, in other words, the application and productive use of information, becomes the business of business.

For Botkin and Davies, knowledge will supersede information just as information has now superseded data.

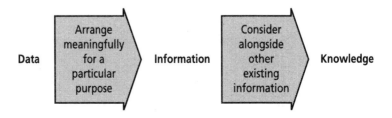

This means that organizations must gain wisdom and knowledge and learn things from all the information that is flying about.

A way of illustrating this change to businesses selling knowledge is through the development of smart products that are able to learn and play a part in the service delivery. We will look at these later in the book.

Another way that you can tell that organizations are moving into the knowledge business is that they're able to customize their offerings based on what they know about customers.

For instance, a telephone credit card will soon know which language you want to use when you call a long distance operator.

In other words, the information age allows businesses to start offering tailored services based on what they know about customers. It is the knowledge that they have about customers which actually is at the heart of the business and is effectively what the businesses sell.

> Another way that you can tell that organizations are moving into the knowledge business is that they're able to customize their offerings based on what they know about customers.

The technical perspective – coded messages

An alternative model draws heavily on the world of telecommunications.

When you use a telephone, you speak – in other words you "send" a "message." This message is "coded" – it is converted into a format that can be sent along telephone lines. It is then "transmitted," before being "decoded" at the other end so that the person listening can "receive" the message. It looks a bit like this:

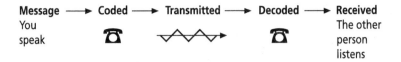

Message ⟶ Coded ⟶ Transmitted ⟶ Decoded ⟶ Received
You ..... The other
speak ..... person
..... listens

In this model, there are several points where things can go wrong and the information can become corrupted. For a start, you may not wind up saying what you mean to say – language is often a poor approximation of meaning. Even if you do say the right thing, there may be an error in coding. During transmission, noise on the line can further corrupt the message. Things may go wrong in the decoding at the other end.

And even if the message does get this far uncorrupted, the listener may misunderstand it – whether because he doesn't understand the language, because he uses words in different ways from you, or because he was expecting you to say something else and did not really listen to what you actually said.

The model has some relevance to information management in general. Information can get corrupted at several points:

● **At source** – the information may be inaccurate, incomplete or misleading;

● **In coding** – for example, information may be typed up inaccurately;

● **In transmission** – it could get lost, or get muddled up on the airwaves;

● **In decoding** – for example, someone may pass on a message to you but leave out vital a element;

● **In reception** – you may read into the information details that are not there.

> The lesson here is: information must be treated with care. What you see may not be what you were sent; what you get may not be what was intended.

■ Modeling data flows

A key development of this perspective is the approach to modeling data flows within an organization. In this approach the argument that, given the many things that can go wrong when information moves from A to B, organizations should take time to map out which information is needed by whom, and then design information systems that ensure that it reaches them in the most efficient manner possible.

This approach is fundamental to the scientific design of information systems. Central to it is the idea of creating "data flow diagrams" which map out the information flows visually and specify exactly what should happen to information at each stage. This approach has the appeal of creating a logical and ordered representation of the organization, with clear scope for control. As information proliferates this can be attractive.

The criticism of the technical perspective is that it may not take sufficient account of the people involved, and the way they may mislay, hold up, hoard, or actively corrupt information. It can lead to information systems that are designed without reference to those who use them and are, therefore, alien and difficult to use – we've all come across them.

The input–output model

One way some organizations have developed of handling the mass of information is to establish a data warehouse which helps to focus the way information comes in and leaves an organization.

This solution seeks to overcome the drawbacks of the technical perspective by bringing together a mixture of people and information technology. Such a system needs real investment in the people and infrastructure and takes some serious planning.

Data warehousing helps organizations to deal with a number of significant challenges. Namely, the need to:

● Project an up-to-date, consistent, and accurate set of information to customers,

● Store and use in a flexible and efficient way the information that the organization generates and receives,

● Use both people and technology to handle and synthesize this information,

● Use the most up-to-date technology solutions available to make sure the information reaches the customer speedily,

● Coordinate all the internal information sources,

● Give staff up-to-date tools to help them use information,

● Replace the vast forest of papers managers have to wade through with sufficient and usable information.

■ Information flow

The first step is to work through a process that allows you to see how information flows in and out of the organization.

The aim is to see how raw information comes into the organization, how it can be translated into useful knowledge for customers, and then how it can be best got to customers in the way they want to receive it.

> The aim is to see how raw information comes into the organization, how it can be translated into useful knowledge for customers, and then how it can be best got to customers in the way they want to receive it.

The eventual objective is to develop a system that works both ways – as a broadcast medium and as a receiving medium (drawing again on the telecommunications analogy). You can get information back from customers and you can give information out to customers in a way they actually want to receive it.

You can do all this by using some of the new information technology that's about to make the job simpler and more targeted.

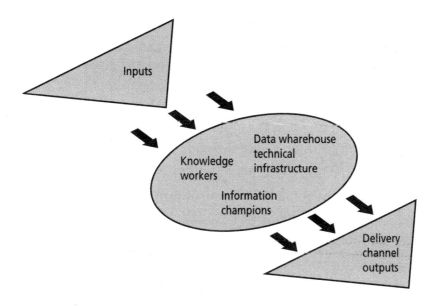

■ Understanding the model

Looking at the model in detail, this is how it might work.

It is important to identify the main generators of information.

These could include:

- Databases held independently – many organizations have separate, singular databases that they use to help run their business.

- The press office. This generates information itself to go to the outside world: press releases, faxes, briefings, and the like, but it also receives a vast amount of information. Information here includes material on trends, cuttings, articles, broadcasts, and such like.

- Another power base in terms of information is management information. This is the kind of information that ends up on both middle and senior managers' desks. It includes market reports, briefings, treasury documents, and the like. Again, this needs to be very up to date and it's a crucial element in the way an organization makes decisions about what to do next.

- The marketing department. There could be a relationship database here, plus of course all the material the company sends out as part of its marketing drives. This includes direct mail, letters, brochures, and so forth.

Basically the inputs can be as broad as possible.

■ The people side

So organizations are likely to have a whole range of what might be called "content providers."

The important thing is to have people in place that understand how to handle information and will work as liaison points between the departments that generate information and the technology.

These are information superworkers and their job is to regularly gather, sift, and prepare the information generated by the content providers. When they have collected this in a consistent format they can enter it into the organization's data warehouse.

The information superworkers will need all the skills we looked at earlier. It's important too that they have an understanding of the work of the different departments from which the information is drawn.

Wise organizations will put a team of people in place here. At the very least, the team needs to include an information technology person, a marketing person, and some stakeholder from senior management.

The job of this team is to pull together the material that's coming from all the content providers, and start to put it into a format that can be used.

In many ways, these people can be seen as gatekeepers of the information system. They take in, they update, they process into a format that can be used further on down the line the information that's available. They also are responsible for setting standards of information so people will know how to present information and what information is actually required in the system.

They are certainly far more than glorified librarians. Their job is to seek out information and liaise with all the providers. They then synthesize it and go about judging its relevance. They also act as standard bearers for the project.

■ The warehouse

The warehouse is really a powerful database.

The people above take in the information regularly and then convert it into a format that can be translated onto this vast database. And whereas in the past this database would probably have taken up a real warehouse or two, nowadays it can just sit in the box in the corner of a room.

And the database includes a vast array of information which is regularly updated. It includes text. This could be brochures, press releases, forms, letters, and the like. It includes pictures. These are standard images and other pictures that are likely to be used.

It can include videos, sound, and animation – all stored on this secure database that can't be broken into or hacked into.

■ The delivery channels

The key is to take all the information and get it out to customers. And there is now a dazzling array of vehicles with which to do this.

The trick is to choose the right vehicle to get the information over. And the range of options will just go on increasing. It certainly beats just sending out a newsletter of doing a poster!

Here are some possibilities:

- **Interactive television.**

- **Multimedia kiosks.** In the future these may even stand on the street rather like 'phone booths. They can have a whole range of uses. Customers can use them to get quotes and information and even sample the service. They don't need staffing and can draw in the curious. They can also dispense information 24 hours a day, every day.

- **Giveaways.** CD disks. These can be included on magazines like consumer magazines and offer customers access to information and maybe games. They are fun and immediate, and great PR.

- **The Internet.** People can find out about products and more. A Web site can be used to cater for younger customers with information about clubs, travel, and book theater tickets, etc. This seemingly extraneous information, on the one hand, creates a sense of belonging for customers, but also allows the organization to sell some of its own products.

> People can also ask questions via the Web site and can be guaranteed an answer within 24 hours.

  People can also ask questions via the Web site and can be guaranteed an answer within 24 hours. It's one of those ways that allows this whole system to be two-way. The organization speaks to customers; the customers speak to the customers.

  And all of it is designed coherently, so the brand remains consistent, as does the company's visual identity.

- **Intranets.** These are internal Internet services that staff can use to find out about developments, and again, to ask questions and receive information.

Intranets

A word about intranets. We believe they are going to be really important elements of the information age. The Intranet is an internal Internet.

It includes company information and can act as a site for feedback and information exchange. Questions from staff can be answered by senior managers and functional specialists.

One way of beginning to establish a culture at work that encourages information sharing is to establish Intranets. The Intranet is an opportunity for employees to tap into the information lifeblood of the organization.

The advantage of Intranets is that they are immediate, flexible, and fun. They can hold vast amounts of information in an accessible and, of course, up-to-date form.

But the Intranet needs to be backed up by a culture that encourages sharing and by browsers which allow effective and understandable access to the information contained.

■ Working on the culture

This kind of program can work but only if the whole culture of the organization supports the free sharing and exchange of information.

This culture needs to overcome the politics of information. The need is to attack four major problems.

1 Information is not available, but managers think it is being deliberately withheld.
2 The information is there but the search engines are unhelpful.
3 People do not know what information is available.
4 Internal politics: People keep information to themselves.

There are ways to overcome this which include the carrot and the stick. The carrots include promotion and bonuses for sharing information. The stick can include taking away all information held by individuals and making it part of a central system.

And, of course, the move to this kind of input–output model

needs to be supported by senior management both in terms of allocating resources and in terms of positive role modeling.

Moving along the virtual value chain

Geoffrey Rayport and John Sviokla again writing in the *Harvard Business Review* came up with another model that may well be useful as we try to see ourselves within a process of change and a process that pushes information and knowledge to the forefront.

To quote Rayport and Sviokla:

Geoffrey Rayport and John Sviokla, *Harvard Business Review*

> Every business today competes in two worlds: a physical world of resources that manages to see and touch, and a virtual world made of information. The latter has given rise to the world of electronic commerce, a new locust of value creation.

In other words, the models we need to see are of organizations moving from a concrete to a more intangible world, and as they do so, getting different value from the information they handle.

In this world organizations gradually move along from seeing information as simply something they handle, to an end in itself – something that adds real value.

For Rayport and Sviokla there are two realms in which organizations operate. These are:

- **The marketplace**, in other words the physical world in which transactions and the like take place, and

- **The market space**, which you might call the more virtual world of an intangible world of information.

They argue that organizations need to integrate these two closely in order to survive in the world as it's likely to be. For the authors, there is a three-stage model. The model shows the way in which organizations have developed and will continue to develop in the new reality that confronts them.

■ Stage 1: visibility

The first stage is what they call **visibility**. In other words, companies are able to look at the way they work and make their operators more effective through analyzing information.

During the last 30 years, many companies have invested heavily in technology and this is being used by companies to help them analyze what they do. It's this steady stream of information that allows organizations to be more effective.

Take the example of Frito-Lay.

Frito-Lay

Frito-Lay is one of the main manufacturers and distributors of food snacks. The company has put in place an information system that allows it to find out, store by store, what products are held and what are required. It collects the information from employees and is able to put it together in a vast computer and then use it to predict stock levels, etc. In other words, the company is still working in the physical marketplace, but is using information to help manage its business more effectively.

■ Stage 2: mirror capability

The second stage in the chain is what Rayport and Sviokla call **mirror capability**. What they mean by this is that organizations need to move from the physical marketplace into the market space – the more virtual information world. In other words, the company needs to make decisions about which parts of their business are more effective at handling this marketplace as opposed to the more traditional way. Organizations are moving their activities from place to space.

An example here is the Boeing company which decided to develop a new 737 aeroplane. In the past, the organization's marketplace activity was building aircraft. This time around though Boeing decided that it wouldn't operate in this realm but would move into the market space. It created a synthetic environment, a mirror world in order to develop its prototype. So they used information, but shifted between realms.

> **Organizations are moving their activities from marketplace to market space.**

■ Stage 3: build new customer relationships

The third stage of the model is where organizations start to **build new customer relationships,** that is when they extract value from this new space that they have begun to understand. Today, thousands of companies now have World Wide Web sites and use them to advertize their products. But the way that people can actually use this new area for the making of new business is especially interesting.

USAA

The example Rayport and Sviokla give is of USAA, a large American insurance company. The company has used this information and is experienced in the market space to broaden it's customer offering. Rather than simply offering insurance, they are now able to offer a wide range of other financial products, shopping services, and the like. In other words, the company has created value from its experience and expertise in the marketplace and market space by reharvesting the information that it already has.

And finally

So you "picks your model, you takes your choice."

What is true is that it is worth thinking through strategies for handling information. But beware, because ideas about information are changing so quickly that these models will quickly look rather out-of-date.

The models can be a useful first step. But we have noticed a worrying trend – organizations tend to get stuck on considering the models and shy away from action.

The models can be a useful first step. But we have noticed a worrying trend – organizations tend to get stuck on considering the models and shy away from action.

The technology may be moving on apace, but many large organizations seem too timid to make a start on using it. *We believe this is because they don't know where to start and are overwhelmed by the possibilities on offer.* So we present a final model to help people move from what's possible to actually starting to harness the awesome power of the information age.

1 **Understand that the new media on offer simply offer you additional communication channels – there is no need to sweep away the existing ones.**

2 **Understand that you will need to experiment in order to get the best from the technology.**

3 **Decide what information you want to receive and send.**

4 **Start your project.**

5 **Test the technology by doing a prototype.**

6 **Do it.**

And a couple of final thoughts. Only use the technology your users have access to. Don't plump for a whizzy technology if users won't be able to access it. And the cost of research and development for the new technologies is often far lower than you might think.

References

Boisot, M. *Information and Organizations: The Manager as Anthropologist*, Fontana, London, 1987.

Broome, A. *Managing Change.*

Davies, S. and Botkin, J. "Coming of knowledge based business," *Harvard Business Review* Sept./Oct.1994.

Keen, J. (ed.) *Information Management in Health Services*. Open University Press, Buckingham, 1994.

Liebenau J. and Backhouse J. *Understanding Information.*

Moss Kanter, R. *When Giants Learn to Dance*, Unwin, 1989.

Rayport G. and Sviokla J. in *Harvard Business Review*, Nov./Dec. 1995.

chapter
four

THERE ARE LOTS OF OPPORTUNITIES ...

- Current developments
- The virtual organization
- Flowering infrastructures
- Growing interdependence
- Learning organizations
- Smart products

It is a safe assumption that
much of what we know today
will be out of date tomorrow

This chapter examines some of the very real changes that have taken place and some of the opportunities available. It begins with a brief survey of some of the new developments in terms of inventions and innovations that are currently happening. It then goes on to look at some of the implications and opportunities available in terms of the way work and organizations are organized.

Some of the key issues we will look at are:

- There are very few "real jobs" any more. Manufacturing now employs less than 20 per cent of the workforce (Employment Department, UK 1994) and this figure will continue declining. More and more people work in information-based jobs within what used to be called the service sector.

  Some two thirds of US employees now work in the service sector, while the Institute for Employment Research in the UK reckons that by the start of the twenty first century nearly 30 per cent of people will be in "data services," gathering, processing, retrieving, or analyzing information.

- There are certainly very few "jobs for life." Traditional lifetime roles are disappearing – there are, for example, 20 per cent fewer secretaries than there were ten years ago. We are moving away from the "career for life" toward what Handy has called "portfolio" working.

  Constant training, retraining, job hopping and even career hopping will become the norm.

- More and more people are on their own. Increasingly, people will work in small firms or as self-employed individuals. This trend looks set to continue as larger employers look increasingly to outsource their staffing.

- It is a safe assumption that much of what we know today will be out of date tomorrow. This is especially true of information

Mary O'Hara-Devereaux and Robert Johansen,
in Global Work, Bridging Distance, Culture and Time

technology, where you can bet your bottom dollar that the machine you buy today will be obsolete by the time you get it home.

All this can be frightening. But it comes laden with opportunity as well.

So we look at:

- current development,
- the growth of virtual organizations,
- the trend toward growing interdependence,
- the flowering of infrastructures,
- the arrival of learning organizations,
- the opportunity to develop "smart" products.

Current developments

In the course of writing this book we became somewhat inundated by information – no surprise there. Articles built up in piles on the floor, books stacked up on shelves, research reports gathered dust and the information age sections in the quality newspapers all added to a general feeling of being swamped.

Still we feel it our duty to report just some of the current developments in this information age. At random we picked some from the pile of material referred to above. The following are just some of the exciting developments on offer. By the time you read this book, some will be reality, some will have been superseded, and there will be a host of new innovations jockeying for our attention.

- A recruitment agency has opened an electronic recruitment fair on the Internet. It is aimed at university/college graduates and major companies that have either already signed up or are negotiating include Pepsi, Nortel, and Asda. The Web site will include information about jobs which applicants can access by clicking a mouse. The site has over 50,000 visits a day and is rising. The method works because it is quick and plugs into just the kind of people the companies are looking for. There are plenty of good graduate Net surfers. Within 15 minutes of being informed of a job, the recruitment agency can have it on the Internet.

- An American scientist is convinced man will communicate with aliens within 10 to 20 years. A new high-tech scanner allows the scientist and his team to analyze 160 million radio channels per second. This is backed up by the world's largest telescope which is 1,000 feet wide and based in Puerto Rico.

- A new monitor can distinguish between real and false contractions. The contraption uses electrodes.

- On the market now is a fax machine that is very small and uses no paper. Designed in Waltham, Massachusetts, it is smaller than a mobile phone and can receive faxes anywhere in the country.

- A robot surgeon that can perform brain operations in space is being developed by NASA. It is the ultimate smart product – a real product of the information age. It is called a Neurosurgical Computational Medicine Testbed. The robot uses a miniature probe attached to a helmet. The robot learns more about the brain as it gains experience. It stores details about tissues and is claimed to be more delicate and accurate than human surgeons. It should be available for use in hospitals on earth within a matter of years.

- The opportunities for educating the young are immense. Youngsters are glued to up-to-date well-designed CD ROMs giving them a world of learning at their fingertips.

- The main banks will soon offer a whole range of services through their customer computers. Using an electronic filofax-type palm top and a modem customers will be able to send checks, order statements, pay bills, and transfer money.

- On the way are personalized newspapers via the Internet. If you don't want overseas news, just get the news you want. As we saw in the last chapter, the ability to customize is one of the major advantages of the information age.

- You can legal advice over the Net.

And this is just a sample of the possibilities. Why not collect a bank of your own examples.

The virtual organization

The first opportunities lie in the new organizations that are being thrown up by the information age. Think of what organizations used to be like. You joined – with a string of paper qualifications – you climbed, you stayed, you retired. You were rewarded for obedience and for toeing the line. Your success was measured by your status and this in turn depended on scrambling up a series of hierarchical ladders.

Not any longer. As Rosabeth Moss Kanter argues, it's now contribution that counts, not status. Organizations need people who contribute, regardless of their job title. And the watchword is flexibility.

■ The driving forces

So what's been driving the change in organizations? It looks like a case of the stick and the carrot. Writers like Charles Handy reflect on the changing environment in which they find themselves – the stick:

Charles Handy,
*The Age of
Unreason*

One thing, at least, is clear – organisations in both private and public sectors face a tougher world – one in which they are judged more harshly than before on their effectiveness and in which there are fewer protective hedges behind which to shelter. It applies to hospitals and schools and employment offices as much as it does to businesses of all sorts.

Moss Kanter describes how, in the face of these pressures, organizations must perform the "ultimate corporate balancing act":

> Cut back and grow. Trim down and build. Accomplish more, and do it in new areas.

Rosabeth Moss Kanter, *When Giants Learn to Dance*

And how do they do it? Peters and Waterman focus on what makes the excellent companies succeed – the carrot:

> More significant, both for society and the companies, these institutions create environments in which people can blossom, develop self esteem, and otherwise be excited participants in the business and in society as a whole.

Tom Peters and Richard Waterman, *In Search of Excellence*

While Bob Garratt argues that:

> Learning is central to the survival and growth of all organizations.

Bob Garratt, *Creating a Learning Organisation*

In other words, organizations have found themselves on a new, more competitive, world stage where their paymasters customers, shareholders, or politicians – expect them to perform ever better and to maintain higher standards of quality. At the same time, they have discovered that the key to survival in this harsher world lies in unleashing the potential of their people, through creating conditions in which they can participate, take decisions, think imaginatively, and be responsible.

To achieve greater flexibility, quicker responsiveness and more attention to quality, organizations are undergoing profound change:

● by flattening hierarchies in order to decrease decision making time,

● by devolving responsibility to teams, and

● by moving closer to the customer.

Indeed the nature of the organization is changing. The traditional bureaucracy is being replaced by looser, more federal structures:

> THE CORPORATION IS DEAD. LONG LIVE THE FEDERATION.

Cable and Wireless poster

And this is why information is now so vital. Bringing in information about the wider, harsher world is vital if we are to follow the changing goal posts around the field. And sharing information within the organization is the linchpin in the new "participate–decide–imagine" culture that organizations must create. If we want our people to think for themselves, we must make sure they have the information and that responsibility for decision making is devolved to them.

from 'Clinical management' by Mark Harrison, Margaret Marion and Andrew Brooks, in *Information Management in Health Services*, edited by Justin Keen, 1994

Indeed, the long-term survival of the devolved organization depends on the effective exchange of information, both vertically and horizontally.

To achieve success the virtual organization will need a cultural shift. People will need to get used to working at a distance. This will not happen overnight.

■ The technological response

These new, more devolved and flexible ways of working are increasingly being supported by use of technologies such as fax, e-mail, and electronic data interchange. Where teams are distributed across several sites, the new technologies can support communication and teamwork without people having to leave their own workplace so frequently (though face-to-face get-togethers still tend to happen – you can't just communicate at a distance).

EDI

Electronic data interchange – or EDI for short – is the key tool for the new age. By using computers, modems, and telephone lines, it's now possible to send and access data at the touch of a button. It means that information can whiz around organizations – the supermarket checkout worker can charge for an item and that item is immediately reordered from the supplier.

And EDI is opening up the world of work:

- British Gas repairmen carry a small portable computer that they can plug into a telephone socket to report faults, order parts, and schedule new visits. With the customer in front of them they can plan how to tackle the problem rather than taking it back to headquarters and wasting precious days in the process.

- The opportunities extend beyond the commercial world. Community nurses can now carry a hand-held computer with patient details. During a visit they can check the record, enter new medication and symptoms. Plugging it into the telephone they can exchange data with doctors or the local hospital.

- Patients in rural areas used to be faced with long journeys if they needed a diagnostic scan. This is now changing. If scans are carried out by a local doctor, they can be sent by fax or modem to a specialist in a distant hospital. Together the specialist and the local doctor can discuss what they see and plan what to do about it.

E-mail

E-mail – short for electronic mail – is one of the vital byproducts of EDI. People can now exchange messages with colleagues on the same site, across sites, and via the Internet across the world. E-mail has its drawbacks – chief among them is a raft of unwanted messages

– but it also offers great potential if well managed. For example:

- To communicate information from the top down – increasingly organizations can use e-mail to update employees about key developments and changes so that everyone knows where they are all the time.

- To report progress up the system – e-mail offers an alternative to the traditional written report.

- To promote internal discussion – for example, at Digital the chief executive answers questions via e-mail, while at Sun Microsystems, e-mail is used to operate suggestion schemes.

- To share information – organizations such as Procter and Gamble use bulletin boards on a range of topics to allow people to ask questions, share ideas, solve problems, etc. Increasingly organizations are using e-mail to facilitate the lateral movement of information so crucial to the new delayered organization.

- To facilitate networking – informal networks can spring up on the e-mail system. These may be mildly subversive – but given the vital role of "skunk works" identified by Peters and Waterman such developments may well be to the long-term good.

Television

It's not just the new flavor of the month and sometime rather cranky technologies that are supporting information sharing. Organizations like IBM are establishing their own internal television network to help people in different sites across the world keep in contact.

> Organizations like IBM are establishing their own internal television network to help people in different sites across the world keep in contact.

Compaq Computer uses television to link up project teams that are distributed across several sites – people on one site can see exactly what their colleagues elsewhere are doing, and hold on-line discussions, make suggestions for improvement, etc.

Indeed, a whole range of conferencing facilities is now available to organizations, from the high-tech, high-grade television network through to the computer bulletin board and down to the humble, but invaluable, telephone conference.

CD ROM

This is probably the best technology with which to distribute information. An ordinary CD ROM can hold 65 MB of information, giving full screen graphics and video. New CD ROMs from IBM can hold 1,000 times as much information.

In future though, the CD ROM may not be with us. As on-line becomes established, the technology will become obsolete!

■ The upshot

The opportunities in all this are many.

- The way information moves around within organizations is changing dramatically with the **flowering of new infrastructures** and indeed whole new views of what an organization is and looks like.

- The exchange of information between organizations is on the increase, with **growing interdependence** in the face of distrust and competition.

- The need for **learning organizations** which can adapt to the changes around them and survive has become essential.

Flowering infrastructures

The traditional information map of an organization reflected the bureaucracy and hierarchy in place. Information moved up (or else!) and down (if you were lucky!). It took its time to do so. And very often it got stuck, either through the complexity of the system or the pigheadedness of middle managers who believed that information was power and, therefore, kept a tight hold on it.

This will no longer do. If teams and individuals are to take their own decisions, react flexibly to change, and be responsible for the quality of the work they do – they need access to information: when they need it, how they need it, and where they need it, and right now – not tomorrow.

The first computerized information systems lovingly aped the timeworn bureaucracies. They cemented the divisions between departments, with "personnel" systems clearly distinct from "payroll" or "quality control." They set in concrete all that was worst about narrow-minded, tribal organizational behavior, proving yet again that information technology is not itself the revolution, even though it may be a tool for the revolutionaries.

These first-wave information systems are now redundant, isolated rocks left behind by the tide of organizational change. The world of work is indeed radically different. No longer must the organization be contained within four walls. The old barriers have been flattened along with the old hierarchies. New information channels are needed inside organizations which reflect the new realities.

- The developments are also supporting the increasing flexibility of work patterns. No longer is the nine to five (or indeed the nine to nine) routine inevitable. Employees can work at home or on the move while keeping in constant touch with their workplace. Who needs to be in the office when you have a video 'phone?

- Homeworking – where individuals and small teams work from an office in their own home – has been given a major boost by the option to exchange data directly across the telephone network. More and more organizations are relying on self-employed consultants for key aspects of their work.

- In the midst of all this we are witnessing the growth of the small partnership – networks of highly skilled professionals on different sites who "meet" together via telecommunications technologies to create small teams and to offer mutual support.

It's even possible that the new technologies and changing ways of working may put an end to the exodus from the countryside that has accompanied the industrial revolution in Europe. Just as the middle classes in the twentieth century fled from the city to the suburbs, the information champion can operate out of the back of beyond. The UK-based Telecottage Association now boasts 129 telecottages across the UK supporting rurally based workers in the remoter parts of the country.

Telecrofting

The traditional Scottish island economy was based on crofting, where people ran smallholdings or "crofts" and supplemented their income with other activities such as fishing. Increasingly the income supplement comes from information activities. To support the growth in rural information workers, in the highlands and islands of Scotland four "telecrofts" have been established in places like Uist in Shetland.

Telecrofts – like their English equivalent of telecottages – are fully wired into the Internet. They provide a range of services including computer and office services, IT training, and access to information about training and qualifications.

Increasingly, information workers in the highlands and islands are directly linked into the information superhighway via modem links, fax, telephone lines, etc.

Growing interdependence

Ask not for whom the bell tolls …

The first major implication of the new environment and the opportunities it presents is the development of new information

> Traditionally, customers screwed suppliers for all they were worth. They set suppliers off against each other.

channels between organizations. No organization can any longer pretend to be an island, immune to the changing world and isolated from the other players around it. Increasingly, organizations must forge partnerships if they are to survive.

■ The new supplier–customer partnerships

Perhaps the most marked change in interorganizational behavior has been the change at the customer–supplier interface.

Traditionally, customers screwed suppliers for all they were worth. They set suppliers off against each other. Central purchasing departments ruled supreme in the overall drive to cut costs – at any cost.

> The modern approach, pioneered by organizations like Marks & Spencer, has been to develop closer relationships with suppliers, indeed to move toward the point where the two organizations work in partnership.

It's become clear that such an approach may cut costs in the short term, but it creates major quality costs in the longer term. Suppliers understood the message to keep costs down – but how? The chances are that they cut back on things that the customer needed, while spending on features that were not required. It was a classic lose–lose situation, where suppliers grudgingly cut back while customers lamented the poor quality of work provided.

The modern approach, pioneered by organizations like Marks & Spencer, has been to develop closer relationships with suppliers, indeed to move toward the point where the two organizations work in partnership. Examples of such partnerships include:

● **Friendlier customer–supplier relationships.** The days of the antagonistic supplier–customer relationship are numbered. Organizations are looking to establish closer ties with key suppliers in order to make sure that suppliers know what matters to them. This may extend as far as contractual relationships laying down the responsibilities of each side.

- **Seeking to influence the way in which suppliers work.** Key suppliers of Marks & Spencer such as Meritina, part of the Coates Vyella group, have radically reorganized their working methods to meet the demands for quality and flexibility that the customer requires. They have moved away from the traditional textile production line toward teamworking, with multiskilled teams in new U-shaped cells which co-operate to try out new designs and assure quality.

- **Working jointly in design teams.** It is just a stage further to set up joint design teams – or at least to involve a supplier representative in the team – to ensure that new products can be produced effectively and to eradicate problems early on.

Partnership in health care

The reforms to the UK National Health Service involved the creation of an "internal market" with **purchasers** – the District Health Authorities which decided what health care was needed in their areas – and **providers** – the hospitals and community care organizations which could provide the care required. The theory of the change was that purchasers might shop around for the services they wanted, creating in the process a leaner, more efficient, health service.

From the outset it seemed unlikely that outright competition would benefit anyone. Increasingly, as Jonathan Shapiro (1994) argues, it became clear that:

> If the NHS is to continue to provide effective, accessible, humane healthcare which is good value for money, it will need to have a shared commissioning framework within which purchasing can take place. Uncontrolled competition is divisive and collusion is corrupting. Collaboration is empowering and inclusive; it should be the watchword of the new NHS.

Examples of collaborative relationships include:

- In Southampton, senior managers from both purchaser and provider organizations meet regularly to build long-term relationships and share each other's strategic thinking.

- In the county of Berkshire the two main providers have positive relationships with the purchasers and are developing joint information systems to support information exchange.

- One purchaser invited information staff from providers to visit and discuss issues, in order to generate cooperation and mutual understanding.

Such partnerships have profound implications for the way in which information is managed.

■ The outward looking organization

It's not just at the supplier–customer interface that things are changing. Increasingly organizations across the spectrum are seeking to redefine their relationships with other organizations, with partnerships flourishing in the place of competition.

Such collaboration is vital in the public sector where, for instance, a problem such as child abuse cannot be tackled effectively by one organization – for example, social services – working alone. Social service departments need to develop partnerships with schools, doctors, hospitals, and so forth to gain a broad picture of what is happening in the community they serve.

But such partnerships are not confined to the public sector. They are becoming more and more common in the world of business, both between complementary organizations and, increasingly, between competitors. Organizations like IBM and Apple can no longer afford to snipe at each other across the barricades – they need to set up joint project teams in areas where cooperation will serve better than competition.

■ Managing at the interface

Such developments have major implications for information management – both for organizations and for managers. They involve a blurring round the edges, with boundaries and frontiers being constantly redefined. Information can no longer be managed in isolation; it must take account of the new partnerships.

> For managers the key challenge is the need to manage at the interface, where boundaries become blurred and loyalties strained.

For organizations, the key challenge is to create interfaces between information systems so that information can move quickly and easily between organizations as it needs to. The new relationships are backed up both by new joint working methods and by electronic data interchange.

For managers the key challenge is the need to manage at the interface, where boundaries become blurred and loyalties strained. But the opportunities to make a real impact increase, as managers strive to influence how their partners behave, and can feed back vital information into their own organization.

We explore in greater detail just what all this involves in the chapters that follow.

Learning organizations

It is the same in a healthy, improving business. All employees, from the CEO to bottom-scale new-hire, get on the path of continuous learning and don't ever get off.

Richard Schonberger, *Building a Chain of Customers*

Organizations must do more than improve the information flows inside themselves, and between them and other organizations. They must radically change the way in which they use the information they have. They must be able to learn, to change, and to grow.

Terms like "learning organization" and "leveraging knowledge" are all the rage. They risk becoming as fashionable as "customer care," "total quality" or "reengineering."

But underlying them is a central truth – that within successful organizations there is a culture which encourages learning. Traditionally, this has often not been the case. As Knasel and Meed (1995) argue:

> We can't assume that learning will take place at work. We have to encourage it. For example, it is important that individuals should be given the opportunity to learn from mistakes rather than to be unfairly castigated for them.

E. Knasel and J. Meed, Becoming Competent: Effective Learning for Occupational Competence

Mike Pedler, John Burgoyne, and Tom Boydell – leading British researchers around the learning organization – suggest that a "learning company," as they call it, should have a number of dimensions:

- **A learning approach to strategy** – in other words, company policy and strategy should be consciously formulated as a learning process.

- **Participative policy making** – all members of the company should have an opportunity to contribute to major policy decisions.

- **Informating** – information technology should be used to empower people; information systems should be open and accessible.

- **Formative accounting and control** – in a similar way accounting and budgetary information should be presented in a way that people can use and learn from it.

- **Internal exchange** – everyone within the company should see themselves and each other as internal suppliers and customers.

- **Reward flexibility** – the assumptions underlying reward systems and structures should be brought out into the open and subject to scrutiny.

- **Enabling structures** – boundaries between departments and functions should be flexible and fluid to enable cross-team working.

- **Boundary workers as environmental scanners** – people with contact with the outside world, such as sales staff, should actively bring information back into the organization.

- **Intercompany learning** – learning companies seek to learn from each other, whether through partnership or benchmarking.

- **Learning climate** – managers create an atmosphere within which everyone is able and encouraged to learn.

- **Self-development opportunities for all** – with appropriate guidance, everyone should be able to take responsibility for their own learning and development.

> Develop teams – teams, with their defined membership, shared sense of purpose, consciousness of being a group and interdependence – can offer the kind of enjoyable, rewarding environment in which learning is more likely to happen.

Knasel and Meed's research highlighted a number of factors that influence the quality of learning which may take place in an organization. In particular, it is important to:

- **Value learning** – there is commitment to employee development from the very top, and this is backed up by resources and time.

- **Create a learning environment** – factors such as how work is organized, the nature of the work that individuals carry out, and how different people work together routinely, all influence the extent to which people learn or fail to learn.

- **Develop learner support skills** – central to success is the way that people help each other to learn, and in particular organizations need to encourage key staff to become effective coaches or mentors.

- **Develop teams** – teams, with their defined membership, shared sense of purpose, consciousness of being a group and interdependence – can offer the kind of enjoyable, rewarding environment in which learning is more likely to happen.

● **Manage the changing role of teachers and trainers** – in the transition toward a learning organization the people most at risk may, ironically, be the trainers. Traditional training was fine for traditional jobs. It is less appropriate to the new realities, where the most important learning takes place on the job, in response to change, development, and mistakes. The role for development professionals is now that of a facilitator, helping people to identify opportunities for learning and to reflect on what they have learned.

> Companies like Coca Cola, Hewlett Packard, General Electric, and US West have employed executives with names like "Chief Learning Officer"

In *Japanese Manufacturing Techniques* Schonberger points out that in the traditional production line people work in a row. Work is "pushed" toward them – often at high speed along a conveyor belt – and they must push it on to the next person on the line. There's little encouragement for learning, especially as errors and mistakes are generally not spotted until quality inspection – when it's too late to make changes.

In many Japanese firms, by contrast, production lines are U-shaped or parallel. Conveyor belts are less common – instead people walk to get work when they need it. Because they "pull" work to them like this any errors are spotted at once by the next person along and together they can try to sort it out. The U-shape means that it's easier for people to move from one job to another and help each other. Learning takes place constantly – mistakes themselves provide learning opportunities and managers will stop the line so the workforce can sort things out, rather than letting problems through.

Quoted in Knasel and Meed, 1995.

More and more organizations are looking to actively create this kind of positive learning environment. Companies like Coca Cola, Hewlett Packard, General Electric, and US West have employed executives with names like "Chief Learning Officer" or CLO. Coca Cola's Judith Rosenblum's job is about:

> Creating and supporting an environment in which learning and applying learning is a daily priority for all of us.

Again, these developments are full of opportunity. Organizations which encourage learning, and managers who facilitate learning, have a future.

Smart products

In their article for the *Harvard Business Review*, Stan Davies and Jim Botkin pointed to the fact that the next wave of economic growth is going to be based on knowledge-based business. There's nothing much new here but along with these knowledge-based businesses, go knowledge-based products. These smart products are likely to have a great impact not just on the way we work, but on the way we learn and indeed on the way we live.

But what do these products look like? Here are just some of the applications that are around at the moment and are likely to be even more popular in the years to come. They are a cautionary note against those who tell us that things aren't going to work out much different from the way they are today.

We need to remember that anything is possible and that these may well just be the start of some pretty extraordinary developments. We've been long accustomed to products that have an element of knowledge. For instance, refrigerators that know when to defrost.

But this is likely to become more and more important. When the clock of a micro-PCM ski jacket senses cold, it turns warm. The same micro-PCMs can be fitted in car seats, curtains, insulation material, and wallpaper.

What about the idea of glass that knows when to reflect or transmit depending on the temperature outside. What about the smart tire that Goodyear has developed which contains a micro chip that can collect and analyze data for air pressure. Eventually this tire may be able to flash a message to the dashboard that tells the driver that the tire pressure is low. You may then tell the driver what to do about it - for instance, if it's in a grand prix race, to take a pit stop. So the first part of the message just conveys simple information, while the second actually shows knowledge. It's a product that will be able to tell you what to do.

References

Davies, S. and Botkin, J. "Coming of knowledge based business" in *Harvard Business Review* Sept./Oct. 1994.

Employment Department. *Labour market and skills trend 1995–6*. Employment Department, Sheffield, 1994.

Handy, C. *The Age of Unreason*, Business Books, 1991.

Harrison, M., Marion, M. and Brooks, A. "Clinical management" in *Information Management in Health Services*, edited by Keen, J.

Garratt, B. *Creating a Learning Organization*, Director Books, 1990.

Knasel, E. and Meed, J. *Becoming Competent: Effective Learning for Occupational Competence*, DfEE, 1995.

Moss Kanter, R. *When Giants Learn to Dance*, Unwin, 1989.

O'Hara-Devereaux, M. and Johansen, R. *Global Work, Bridging Distance, Culture and Time*.

Pedler, M., Burgoyne, J. and Boydell, T. *The Learning Company*, McGraw-Hill, 1991.

Peters, T. and Waterman, R. *In Search of Excellence*, Harper Collins, 1982.

Schonberger, R. *Building a Chain of Customers*.

Schonberger, R. *Japanese Manufacturing Techniques*.

Shapiro, J. "A time to share" in *Health Service Journal*, 104:5427 (1994).

chapter five

BEHAVIORAL SKILLS FOR THE INFORMATION AGE

While certain gateway skills are needed to use new technology and to talk to propeller heads, the crucial skills are behavioral and interpersonal

Introduction

So far in this book we have flagged up some of the key opportunities and challenges that the information age has brought with it. We have looked both at the changing technologies and at the radical developments in organizations and how they work.

But what does this mean for managers? In particular, what are the behavioral skills that people will increasingly need to survive in the information age? This chapter and the next explore some of the key skills that we think will be especially important. Both chapters are based on the premise that while certain gateway skills are needed to use new technology and to talk to propellor heads, the crucial skills are behavioral and interpersonal.

The challenges

We begin by discussing the challenges that information champions will face, in the process summarizing some of the key issues in the early chapters. The principle challenges include:

- Needing to manage on the basis of competence rather than status,
- Needing to manage at the interface between organizations,
- Needing to manage with reduced levels of certainty, in the face of ambiguity and change,
- Needing to manage the new technologies,
- Needing to learn the art of the possible.

In all these cases we use the word "manage" in both its senses. We need to be able to manage in the sense of surviving or coping in the face of challenge and change. But we also need to be able to manage in the more active sense of influencing the new realities for the benefit of ourselves and our organizations.

So the basic gateway of entry operates through a mixture of thinking and doing. It is about skills and attitudes. The two cannot be strictly divorced.

■ Managing on the basis of competence

Before the information age, managerial authority was based on status and position within the organization. In traditional organizations managers were principally expected to control work and could expect obedience from their staff regardless of how well or badly they themselves performed.

However, things have changed. As Rosabeth Moss Kanter argues:

Rosabeth Moss
Kanter
*When Giants Learn
to Dance*

> Status, not contribution, was the traditional basis for the numbers on people's paychecks. Pay was cemented to hierarchical position, regardless of performance. But this system does not square well with the new business realities.

The new business realities that Moss Kanter mentions include in particular the move away from traditional bureaucracies toward less hierarchical or matrix structures, and the increasing importance of self-managing teams. All these mean that managers can no longer rely on hierarchical authority, they must manage on the basis of competence and respect.

Some of the challenges here are:

Competence must be reaffirmed

Managers must change and adapt with the times. They must rise to the new challenges and demonstrate that they are still capable of doing their job. Fundamentally, this means that we must be good learners.

The growth of leadership

"Managing" tended to stress activities such as planning, monitoring and controlling work. Such activities remain important – but they now form a much smaller part of the manager's role. Increasingly, managers must also be able to "lead" – to provide vision, to inspire, to set an example, to carry people forward.

The importance of teamwork

Working in teams also has vital implications. As Belbin (1981) has argued, the manager as team member may need to play several roles – not just as leader but as supporter, ideas generator, etc.

However, while these challenges are important, they also present crucial opportunities. The days of the manager stuck in his or her office issuing orders and carrying the can are gone. We are now free to work to our full potential.

■ Managing at the interface

Chapter four highlighted the ways in which organizations must increasingly forge partnerships with their customers, suppliers, collaborators, and even with their competitors. As collaborative ventures take root, increasing numbers of managers must work at the interface between their own organization and their partner organizations.

Managing across the boundary brings a new and varied set of challenges:

A question of identity

These developments place demands on managers that run counter to much that we expect. As Margaret Wheatley argues in *Leadership and the New Science* we tend to believe that:

> To maintain our identity, we must protect ourselves from the demands of external forces. We tend to think that isolation and clear boundaries are the best way to maintain individuality.

This comfortable sense of identity may be challenged.

Margaret Wheatley, *Leadership and the New Science*

A question of loyalties

Working between organizations can bring traditional loyalties into question. Spending time with other organizations can blur a manager's responsibilities and indeed the manager's perception of his or her role.

> One manager we knew played a key role in promoting his organization to the wider world. He was held in high esteem and was undoubtedly responsible for raising the organization's profile and indirectly bringing in important work. However, this laid him open within the organization to the criticism that he spent too much time working with and on behalf of other organizations, and not enough on other aspects of his work.

More and more, managers face this kind of dilemma. It can become increasingly difficult to please all of the people all of the time. It is important to accept this, not to pretend it doesn't exist.

Public face, private person

Managers at the interface also have to consider the image of themselves that they project. Do they project the same persona to the outside world as they do to people within the organization? If not, how do they handle the joins?

Once again, these challenges bring opportunities. Wheatley also argues that, if we can confront the need to look beyond boundaries, this will bring clear benefits:

Margaret
Wheatley,
*Leadership and
the New Science*

Openness to environmental information over time spawns a firmer sense of identity, one that is less permeable to externally induced change. ... In the world of self-organizing structures, we learn that useful boundaries develop through openness to the environment. As the process of exchange continues between the system and the environment, the system, paradoxically, develops greater freedom from the demands of its environment.

In other words, the organization benefits from having contacts with the outside world because this provides a gateway for information. It means that, if we can develop the appropriate skills to work effectively at the interface, we can help the organization to become more influential and more active in the face of change.

> The first paradox of the information age is that, while the deluge of information grows by the day, we must increasingly take decisions on the basis of insufficient information.

It's worth reflecting back to the open systems approach described in chapter three. If organizations do to some extent behave like living organisms, adapting to and seeking to modify the environment around them, then the points of contact with that environment will be crucial to the organization's ability to evolve and survive.

■ Managing with uncertainty

> We are entering an age of unreason … a time when the only prediction that will hold true is that no prediction will hold true.

Charles Handy,
The Age of Unreason

The first paradox of the information age is that, while the deluge of information grows by the day, we must increasingly take decisions on the basis of insufficient information. The rule book goes out of the window as we need to take decisions without the benefit of experience, knowledge, and procedure.

We are also becoming increasingly aware that the rational model – where we try to reduce a complex, multidimensional reality to a simple linear formula – will no longer work. We need to accept that the world is, in Tom Peters' words, "messy"; that we

> It has been said that the only human who likes change is a baby with a wet bottom.

must make the most of the ambiguity and complexity that surrounds us, not pretend that everything is simpler than it really is.

It has been said that the only human who likes change is a baby with a wet bottom. This may have a ring of truth to it, but change and flexibility are at the base of any entry to the new information age.

Peter Brownlow,
senior
marketing
manager with a
large US
transportation
carrier

"I remember when our chief executive gave a talk. He explained that many of the old certainties were gone and that we had to accept change as the new way of the world. His actual words were that we were in a truly chaotic world and this had to be understood and that we needed to thrive on it.

He said he would lead us to the edge of the precipice, but it was up us to jump off. That jumping off was how it is, but that we would come to no harm. He was really saying that we all have to deal with uncertainty."

Some of the key challenges here include:

Accepting the limits to planning

While we can – and indeed must – plan what we intend to do, we must also recognize that our plans are only approximations of what will happen. They, therefore, need to be sufficiently flexible to enable us to respond openly to change and development:

Margaret
Wheatley,
*Leadership and
the New Science*

I can think of several organisations, particularly market-oriented ones, that brag about how a customer inquiry or the suggestion of an employee directed them into new product lines that became very successful. There was no pre-planning, no long-range strategic objectives, that led them into these markets. Just the creativity of one or a few individuals who succeeded in getting the attention of the organization and then watched the process amplify itself into a new, unexpected direction for the company.

Tom Peters and Nancy Austin (1985) take up the theme when they talk about "skunkworks – those small off-line bands of mavericks that are the hallmark of innovative organizations."

Learning the benefits of mistakes

We must be prepared to take decisions that will be wrong – and accept that other people will take wrong decisions as well. This is not a charter for sloppy decision making – it is instead a plea for allowing sufficient flexibility to be able to learn from what happens and to influence events if necessary. We must accept fallibility.

Bill Gates, head of Microsoft, is reported to have said that he would refuse to employ any manager who had not made some major mistakes. The reason? Because mistakes may show that someone is prepared to experiment, take risks, go out on a limb.

It is difficult to accept, but strict perfectionists will not gain access to the information age. It is messy; it is overwhelming and mistakes are inevitable.

The limits of objectivity

Things will increasingly become harder to measure, at least in hard, objective ways. Can we, for instance, go on using balance sheets that do not allow for intellectual capital? Can we go on rewarding staff for work but not for learning?

> It is difficult to accept, but strict perfectionists will not gain access to the information age. It is messy; it is overwhelming and mistakes are inevitable.

Once again, much of this is good news once we face up to it. How many times have you felt, after the event, that you could have done something better if only you had had the freedom to follow a new idea through? That freedom is now here.

■ Managing the new technologies

From the development of printing to the arrival of the personal computer, literacy – and to a certain extent numeracy – were the basic skills that were essential for access to information and indeed to society in general. Writers like Freire (1972) and Hoggart (1958) highlighted not just the importance of basic literacy in social integration, but also the ways in which patterns of literacy could be used to maintain or to modify power structures.

Hoggart in particular has pointed out how changes in literacy have important implications. At the end of *The Uses of Literacy* he argues:

R. Hoggart,
*The Uses of
Literacy*

The fact that illiteracy as it is normally measured has been largely removed only points toward the next and probably more difficult problem.

Increasingly basic computing skills are themselves becoming keys for entry into society, as important as being able to read and write. Who needs a dictionary when they have a spellchecker? Who needs tables when they have a calculator? Children growing up today are – or should be – acquiring these skills as a matter of course. For many managers, however, they are new, alien, and demanding.

So the arrival of computers poses two additional challenges to the manager in the information age:

- **A new literacy.** We need to learn to become as at home with computers to access, record, store and communicate information as we have been with pen and ink.

- **A new oral tradition.** In addition, we need to be able to talk about computers effectively. In particular, we need to be able to communicate our needs and problems to information specialists who may have a language and world view radically different from our own.

No one needs to become a nerd or a propeller head, just as no one needed to write like Shakespeare to survive in the age of literacy. We do need to demand the keys to the new kingdom.

And, just as Hoggart was concerned that the growth of popular publications brought with it its own set of concerns – "the dubious quality of life such things promote" – so today's self-proclaimed guardians of morality are anxious that the growth of the Internet raises new dilemmas of censorship and freedom.

The skills

The challenges we have described call for a new set of skills in managers. And, surprisingly perhaps for a book with the word "information" in the title, very few of these skills relate directly to computers. Most of them center around the way we behave and relate to other people and around coping in the new environment.

Thinking back to the example of the US military in our introduction, we can't expect people to passively accept orders in quiet and temperate workplaces. These days workplaces are often noisy and suffering from data overload. We need to learn to manage this.

For the purposes of this book we have divided the key personal skills into two broad categories:

- **Gateway skills:** this is where the technology focused skills such as understanding computers and talking to information specialists come in. They are the basic keys we need to access the information age.

- **Champion skills:** while we need gateway skills to gain access to the information age, we need a rather different set of skills to survive in it. We need, for example, to be able to use information sources, to sift through information effectively, to take decisions in the absence of certainty and to learn continually from our experience.

Above all we need to make the most of the opportunities that accompany the new challenges. This calls for networking and benchmarking skills, the ability to help others to learn and to work effectively in the self-managing team.

The gateway skills

The key gateway skills are becoming – and remaining – familiar with developments in the new technologies, and communicating with specialists.

No new technology skills, no entry.

Saj Arshad,
Visa
International

The current basic entry point to the information age in Visa is to be familiar with Windows. You don't need much more than that because the interfaces are common and easily understood. However, I feel that the dominance of this environment will change. In the future it is going to be Intranets that are really going to start dominating organizations. In fact we're already seeing it happen in many multinational organizations.

Getting to grips with the new technologies

The first thing to be clear about is that we don't all have to become computer whiz kids. We need to be able to use and manage the new technologies in order to fulfill the wider vision we have of our role and the developments within our organization.

Krishnan Shanta
Kumar, Director
of Corporate
HRD at India's
Raymond
Woollen Mills.
Quoted in
"How IT is
changing the
way you
manage," in
*World's
Executive Digest
Technology,*
September
1995.

Today, I can't take a decision without my computer. My daily routine is computer-based. For me, managing without a computer is like being a doctor without a stethoscope. New user-friendly and tailor-made software packages have made information available to me quickly, and this has made decision-making easier. There has been a drastic reduction in my dependence on gut feel.

It's all in the mind

Perhaps the most difficult thing about the new technologies is just that – they are new, and as a result unfamiliar. What's more, the first computers were highly unfriendly and difficult to use. It's easy to think that you won't be able to understand them, or that even if you do, you'll lose all your work at the press of a key, or expose vital secrets to the outside world.

We need to understand some of the basic ways computers "think." This means if a computer decides to act oddly or doesn't do what you want it to then you can think your way around the problem and make it do what you want it to. This comes with time, but you should always be looking to get inside the "mind" of your computer.

The first step is to confront this mind set. In practice, most people can come to terms with the new technology, quite easily. Nowadays there is no need to work with inaccessible programs. We can all demand a user-friendly work environment within which we can feel at home and at ease.

> Nowadays there is no need to work with inaccessible programs. We can all demand a user-friendly work environment within which we can feel at home and at ease.

> "When I started we all felt like we were walking on egg shells. There would be anguished cries from around the office as a computer crashed and people would lose a day's work. It really isn't like that now. Everything is much easier. We use the Mac and you just don't lose work as you used to."

Ian Hare,
Godfrey Davis,
Car Hire

It's certainly no problem for the new generation which is more at home on a computer than in front of a book. As one senior manager memorably said to us:

> "My 12-year-old daughter knows more about computers than many of the people here."

Peter Fenton,
CDC Associates

And this means that today's managers really do need to put aside the fears and prejudices of the past, as these will be no obstacle to the information champions of the future.

> "We can't let the technology get in our way and prevent us from taking part in the revolution. No longer do we need programming experts to handle the data. A Visa employee can now handle incredible data. They can interrogate the software in a way that just a few years ago would have been impossible."

Saj Arshad,
Visa International

Deciding what role you wish to play

So the first key step is to decide what role you wish to play. It's possible to identify four possible roles, as shown in the table overleaf.

All these roles are legitimate and valuable. Which you play will depend on your preferences, your work, your organization and the support available to you. Having a clear vision of where you want to go is however vital, and being able to express this vision is key.

Role	Description	Example
User	The user is possibly the most basic role. At this level you will identify the tools that can help you do your job effectively – for example, using word processors, spreadsheets, etc. to prepare reports, or using networks to communicate with colleagues elsewhere in or beyond the organization.	General practitioners using e-mail to communicate with colleagues request results of tests, join bulletin boards for their own areas of interest.
Influencer	The influencer will seek to ensure that his or her team has the best tools to support them in their work. To do this they will need to be aware of what's available and what it can do. They will also need to be skilled at making a case. They may not be users themselves.	A manager who works closely with the information department to make sure her team gets the most appropriate networking software.
Advocate	The advocate will seek to influence how the wider organization uses the new technologies. This will involve creating or supporting a vision and strategy, encouraging, helping and supporting other people, and lobbying for resources.	A manager pushing for direct links with suppliers via networking and shared software.
Expert	The expert is someone who knows enough about the new technologies to be able to design systems, buy in hardware and software, etc. All too often, experts stand outside the normal line management structure.	An enthusiastic manager who gets fully involved in planning and setting up information systems.

Auditing what you have

Another key step to take is to audit the systems and technologies that you have in place to check how well they meet your requirements. You need to ask questions like these:

- *Do you receive quality information – the right information, when and where you need it, in the right form? Is the information you receive presented appropriately? How much vital information doesn't get to you?*

- *How effectively used is the information you provide to other people? Could it be used for other purposes? Would the information be useful for other people?*

- *How accessible is the system? Could more people use it? Could it be simplified or made more user friendly? Could more or better training and instructions be provided?*

- *Where does information get stuck? What are the points where it disappears from view? Are these at the edge of the organization? At boundaries between departments or teams? At points in the hierarchy?*

You and your team have a right to receive the information you need to do your job. You also have a responsibility to make sure you give other people the information they need.

What's more, the systems you use are often the biggest barriers to becoming familiar and feeling at ease with new technologies. If your computer screens flash up incomprehensible messages, get them changed. These days GUIs (graphical user interfaces) mean that everyone should be able to navigate a system easily, regardless of how much they know about it.

Keeping in touch with what's available

Much useful technology is now available. And the range increases daily. You need to keep up to date with the resources that might support you, your team, and your organization. Ways of doing this include:

- Developing a good relationship with experts (see next section) to ensure that they keep you posted about developments of interest.

- Using published resources – these can include journals in your own area of work, computer pages of newspapers, computer magazines, etc.

> Get wired – join computer networks, bulletin boards, etc. that can help you keep up to date.

- Getting wired – join computer networks, bulletin boards, etc. that can help you keep up to date.

Learning more

Above all, you need to identify someone who can help you learn effectively about new technologies. Far too many people get sent on computer courses where they learn nothing. You need to find someone who:

- Is genuinely sensitive to your needs and prepared to tailor what they offer to suit you;

- Works in a way that suits your learning style;

- Is prepared to coach you, answering questions as you learn and providing constructive feedback;

- Can talk in a straightforward way without using unnecessary jargon;

- Doesn't load you down with knowledge that is of no use to you now or in the future.

These people do exist.

A graphic designer we know found standard training courses in using page layout packages of little value. The person he found most useful lived locally, was happy to be phoned up at odd times, and came out to sit with him while he got the hang of the system. Most usefully, he offered sound advice about which program was most likely to meet our colleague's own, individual needs.

■ Communicating with information specialists

Communicating with the specialists involves several key things:

- Knowing what you want,
- Knowing how to ask for it,
- Knowing the basic vocabulary.

Knowing what you want

This is the vital thing. It's like with buying a car or having your kitchen fitted out. If you go into a car sales room without knowing what you need, you're likely to buy something you don't want. If you call out the kitchen installers without getting your own needs straight, they won't be able to offer you adequate advice.

You don't need to understand how cars work before you buy one. You don't even need to know all the jargon – turbo-powered, twin carbs, etc. In just the same way you don't need to know which joints the carpenter will use, or the name of the wax he or she may apply. What you must know is what you want the car or the kitchen to do for you.

It's just the same with computers and telecommunications. Forget binary code, gigabytes, dots-per-inch, COBOL, or BASIC. You don't need to know any of it and if you find a specialist using it, tell them to stop.

What you must get clear is what you want the technology to do for you. You want to get a message out to 20 sites simultaneously – that's fine. You want your sales people to be able to contact you night and day – great. You want to produce documents to a particular standard – fine. The technology can do all this and far more.

> **What you must get clear is what you want the technology to do for you.**

So you need to start with a vision. Put aside all the preconceptions you have about how information can be organized. Open your mind, get creative, and imagine the world you want to live in. Better still, do it with your team – that way you get four times more ideas and an even better vision.

Then, turn your vision into something tangible. Write down as precisely as you can what you want to happen, to what standard, and at what speed. Put priorities on your needs. Then, you can start to talk with the specialists.

Knowing how to ask for it

Once you have established a clear vision, you are in a position to talk to specialists about it. Explain your vision clearly. If they think it's difficult to do something, ask them why. Look for compromises and alternatives together. Above all, be assertive. You are the customer, and they have a duty to meet your needs.

- Ask questions to check that you've understood. Don't feel that you have to pretend to understand everything they say – ask them to explain terms or ideas that are unfamiliar. Key questions include:

  "Can you put that another way?"

  "I haven't quite followed that. Could you go over it again?"

  "But if we do XYZ, will we still be able to get messages out to suppliers the same day?"

  "Can I just check that I've got that. If we do ABC, then XYZ will happen. Is that right?"

- Check that they have understood as well. Your own activities may be as alien to them as theirs are to you. So be prepared to explain things again, in a different way.

Knowing the basic vocabulary

It is important to work through the basic vocabulary. But first make sure you are clear about some basic concepts:

- information management,
- information systems,
- information technology.

Now some of the key contexts:

- personal computing,
- networks, large and small,
- electronic mail,
- the superhighway,
- etc.

Finally, a whistle stop tour through the labyrinth of uses:

- word processing,
- spreadsheets,
- communications packages,
- databases,
- works packages,
- desk top publishing,
- computer-aided design,
- simulations,
- virtual reality,
- etc.

■ The art of the possible

It is all too easy to get carried away by the possibilities on offer. The basic gateway skills include the ability to consider the possibilities on offer and make realistic choices.

Too much pie in the sky and you'll lose credibility. So the basic gateway means keeping abreast but keeping feet on the ground.

A letter from the information age

David Wynne-Owen, senior brand services manager at TSB, a large UK bank, explains how he entered the information age.

David Wynne-
Owen, Senior
Brand Services
Manager, TSB

What is the information age?

The way to define the information age is to do so in terms of what it means to managers.

In this age managers need to quickly understand what all the information means. They need to gain understanding out of what is basically an information overload. Paper, CD ROM disks, the Internet and Intranet mean you can search for a topic and you can just get a thousand documents to look through.

What's going to happen is that with the more total search utilities you'll be able to refine your interests almost by speaking to the computer which will actually make life easier.

One of the things the information age is characterised by is the vast amount of information we receive. Just thinking about an average week in my working life and I'm likely to receive internal corporate circulars, news letters, information via agencies, direct mail, magazines, computer magazines. You get all this paper-based material. I'm also finding that as a topic comes up I search on one of these search engines and a whole array of information comes through there. I regularly search Compuserve and we just get lots and lots of information. We also get CD ROM samplers.

Current developments

I'm currently working on designing interactive TV and I think we'll see that in future we'll be getting an information overload at home too. Just think of the fact that people already do have literally hundreds of TV channels available to them. It's actually going to be very difficult to decide which information is important and I think this is one of the defining characteristics of this information age.

What's interesting is that people will spend more and more time at home. There'll be home banking, the Internet, education over the Internet. It's fascinating really to think that the whole shape of society may change.

Actually the interesting thing is I'm both sceptical about the information age and very excited about it. I get very excited about what's possible, but you have to put a practical view point on this. You need to constantly ask how much you actually need of what's available and what we're actually doing right now. The important thing is picking up the best of the information age and what it offers us rather than simply searching for the new.

What's interesting is that continually you find there are new ways of doing things – new software utilities, new electronics, new DTP packages. These days we're using large storage devices, CD ROM and a whole range of new multi-media products. These include multi-media kiosks and home banking through the PC. The interesting thing is that as soon as you think you've crowned an area it changes again and there's a whole new range of possibilities. On the one hand, it's frustrating, but also it's extremely exciting.

One of the real trends we've noticed is the ability to customise. We're able to use our interactive kiosks to actually develop personalised quotes for people, and ten years from now it'll be quite normal for a kiosk to do everything in banking. People may never go into an actual bank.

The manager of the future

The manager of the future's job is going to be completely bound up with what's possible with new computer-type vehicles. All managers will need to understand why customers buy, what they're interested in, and customer information requirements. They'll have to turn this knowledge on its head and understand how you need to use the computer's processing power to bring this in an interesting and informative way to the customer. In other words, they'll have to take the key disciplines of their job and apply the technology to really make it happen. They won't need to be real boffins, but they will need to use the new technology.

Some key skills

I think to really understand the skills sets that are needed I'd like to say something about the way I've moved along in this world. Essentially you must have an interest in computers and more than just using a simple spreadsheet. You need to have some idea of how a gadget might work - button X makes this happen and so on. You need to understand the basic logic of computers.

My interest was sparked about 8 or 10 years ago when I started working with my first PC to put together evaluation spreadsheets. I got really interested in the technology then and started to think how this essentially was a big calculator, and how it could help me come up with an answer that would allow my boss to approve what might be a £2,000,000 spending package. You must be interested in exploring. You must be inquisitive. You need to, if possible, push it to its limits.

From what was basically a simple calculator I moved into marketing. And it was here that I got interested in Apple Macs. I got interested in them because the interface was so easy to understand. I had fewer technology skills than others and the Mac really allowed me to look like a whizzo on the technology. I found that I could learn more because of the graphical interface. I then started becoming interested in other packages. I did some work on DTP packages, photo manipulation packages, video manipulation - for fun.

It's important to say that I'm not a designer or able to redesign something in detail, but I understand the packages and it was through this experimenting and working with the more complex packages that I really started to get more confident. You don't need to be a designer or a computer person. What you need is an understanding of the thinking behind these ideas.

So the key is to keep being inquisitive and keep learning and this seems to me to be the real passport for the information manager of the future. It's important also not to be frightened of the terminology. Every time you meet somebody who uses a new word ask what it means. It's when you speak the language that the consultants use that you really start getting ahead.

In the future I don't think it's beyond the bounds of possibility that people will be walking around with portable laptops within their wrist watches. These may well allow them to, through voice, touch or e-mail, access a whole range of services amongst which may be the ability to shop.

One of the most important developments is going to be the Intranet. This will give us access to product features and buckets of corporate information. It will be a data warehouse of all the graphics, text, video, and everything that we'll be able to use. This seems to me to mean that we may well be able to work from home and put together whole portfolios of information.

And what about the information manager of the year 2000? Well for a start they're going to have to be flexible. Old job definitions are going to break down. People will be expected to do a far wider range of things. The manager then won't be frightened of technology. He or she will be inquisitive and always looking to find out more. The manager of the year 2000 will be the person that manipulates data, turns it into information, and then uses it to make decisions.

References

Belbin, M. *Management Teams: Why they Succeed or Fail*, 1981.

Freire, P. *A Pedagogy of the Oppressed*, Penguin, Harmondsworth, 1972.

Handy, C. *The Age of Unreason*, Business Books, 1991.

Hoggart, R. *The Uses of Literacy*, Penguin, 1958.

Morris, S., Willcocks, G. and Knasel E. *How to Lead a Winning Team*, Pitman, London, 1995.

Moss Kanter, R. *When Giants Learn to Dance*.

Peters, T. and Austin, N. *A Passion for Excellence*, Fontana, 1985.

Wheatley, M. *Leadership and the New Science*.

"How IT is changing the way you manage," in *World's Executive Digest Technology*, Sept. 1995.

chapter
six

SURVIVAL SKILLS FOR THE INFORMATION CHAMPION

Tomorrow there will be no more managers. There will only be leaders – leaders who constantly reaffirm their competence and gain support from their people through the example they set and the way they treat people

"The real information champions are probably still at school. This generation is just laying the foundations. Even the stars of today are living on borrowed time."

Neil Svensen

Introduction

In the information age it is tempting to believe that the key personal skills will involve using computers and telecommunications systems. And as we saw in the last chapter, such skills do have a basic role to play in ensuring access to the new age.

However, the fundamental skills for the information champion do not involve connecting wires or pushing buttons; they are very much personal and interpersonal skills. They may involve using technology, but only as a medium or a channel for communication.

The key skills to survival that we believe information champions will need are:

- Using information sources effectively,
- Sifting through the wealth of information,
- Taking decisions on the basis of uncertainty,
- Communicating information widely,
- Championing learning,
- Networking skills.

These are a passport to success.

In the last chapter we received one "letter" from an information champion, David Wynne-Owen. Later in this chapter we receive another from Saj Arshad of Visa International. But let's start with a briefer "postcard" from Paul Dickinson, new business director at a design company.

> ### Come on in, the water's fine
>
> *What most excites me is that the information revolution gives us the opportunity to live different lives. Because we can do so much, using the new technology from home, we don't need to spend our time sitting in sweaty traffic jams and offices.*
>
> *But to enter the world I feel there are three main things you need:*
>
> *1 In an environment that is changing at a scary pace where no one knows exactly what will happen you need to get experience. You need to be close to any new developments and make an effort to constantly gain experience.*
>
> *2 You need to deal with the vast array of information.*
>
> *3 You need to champion your knowledge. You need to be able to explain clearly what opportunities there are and why you are doing things. The need to make things clear has never been more important. And it's through clarity and not jargon that you gain credibility.*

■ The key question is why

Mike Bartram,
Consumer
Congress

Far more managers can tell you HOW they provide information and HOW they consult, than WHY they do it. The real information revolution will come only when managers and politicians can show greater commitment to change and sharing power; and a greater understanding of how to build this commitment into the blood stream of organizations. Until then, the opportunities of the superhighway are likely to remain largely elusive.

When Josiah Wedgewood opened his pottery factory in the eighteenth century he also opened the door to the industrial revolution. And the first thing the workers saw as they came through that door and into the factory was a lovely thick book of rules.

The industrial revolution was indeed founded on rules. The role of the manager was to plan, monitor, and control. The developing production lines took this to extremes – following the ideas of Taylor, work was organized in as logical a manner as possible. Workers were discouraged from thinking – it was the managers who had to do the thinking for them, and then to put the thinking into rules, policies, and procedures.

Think about what we now need from information workers. We need their ideas. We need them to bring information in from outside. We need them to spot and solve problems. We need them to delight existing customers and bring in new customers. We need their enthusiasm and commitment.

The dumb worker has been replaced by the dumb terminal. The really mundane, routine tasks can be done by machines, and nowadays everyone must be able to think. This means that organizations can no longer live by rules alone – they must manage by consent, because they need so much more from their people. And the information champion will need to help the organization rewrite the rule book – or indeed to throw it away altogether.

Tomorrow there will be no more managers. There will only be leaders – leaders who constantly reaffirm their competence and gain support from their people through the example they set and the way they treat people.

Above all, the leaders of tomorrow will ask why. Why do we do things like this? Why do we say that won't work here? Why do we have that form? Why is that procedure like it is? Why do we put up with information like that? Why don't we share more?

Using information sources effectively

In the age of information overload, who needs information sources?

The answer is – we all do. Good information sources can actually

help to reduce information overload by providing quality information that is fit for the purpose you intend to put it to.

■ Quality information

Quality information is:

- **Relevant.**
- **Clear** – you can understand it; it does not contain unnec-
  essary jargon.
- **Timely** – you receive it when you need it – not too soon so
  it can go out of date or above all too late to be of use.
- **Accurate** – fitness for purpose is important here; quality
  information is *accurate enough* for your purposes.
- **Sufficient** – there is enough information, without it being
  excessive.
- **Reliable** – you can have confidence in it.
- **Targeted** – it goes to the right person, via an appropriate
  channel and in an appropriate format.
- **Worthwhile** – the benefits it provides outweigh the costs of
  obtaining it.

Quality information can have many benefits.

- It can save you time (and possibly money, though you may not
  mind paying more for quality information). Good information
  sources are effective at obtaining the information you need
  and do it more efficiently than you would yourself.

- It can help you to make better decisions. Information is crucial
  to decision making. Having the right information at the right
  time means that you can develop a wider range of possible scenarios, explore the implications of each and assess the likely
  impact of each course of action.

● More intangibly perhaps, it can make you more aware of likely changes, trends, and developments. For example, if you can rely on a member of the sales team to bring in relevant information about what customers think about your products, you can be confident that you will become aware of possible changes in customer preferences promptly.

Robert Chandran, CEO of US-based Chemoil Corporation, describes how one key information source – news wire services – help him to compete with Shell, Exon, Chevron, and other big oil companies.

> News wire services are tremendously helpful. They provide me with the information I need to compete with these companies head-on.

Quoted in "How IT is changing the way you manage," in *World's Executive Digest Technology,* September 1995.

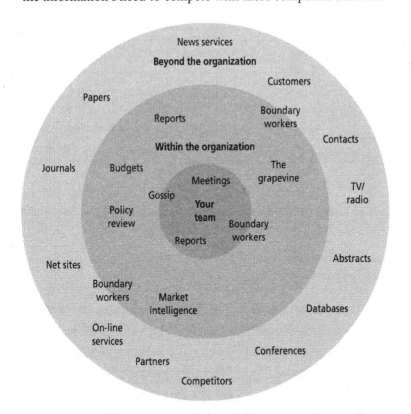

Information sources may be within your own team – the people you work with on a day-to-day basis. The quality of information you receive from your team is critical. They may be elsewhere in the organization. Or they may be outside the organization, as the diagram on page 129 shows.

The diagram helps to bring out some key issues around information sources. These issues are crucial to a proper understanding of information sources, and to making the most of them.

■ Maximizing informal sources

Firstly, some information sources are much less formal than others. Contacts with customers, partners, and colleagues in other organizations, along with the grapevine and gossip mongers within the organization, can be as important as the more formal sources like journals or on-line services.

> People like sales staff, project workers, and others with regular contacts with the outside world represent a crucial chanel of information into the organization; meetings, formal and informal, can have similar functions.

The first key point with using information sources is to cultivate these contacts. They are generally free, they tend to provide information that is clear and easy to understand and they may be timely.

On the down side you need to assess the information from them carefully. Assessing it against the checklist for quality information, it may not be sufficient, accurate, or reliable. In many cases it will be one ingredient, which you need to test out alongside information from other sources.

■ Valuing interfaces

Secondly, many fertile sources of information exist at the boundaries. People like sales staff, project workers, and others with regular contacts with the outside world represent a crucial channel of information into the organization; meetings, formal and informal, can have similar functions. It's again crucial to cultivate these interface contacts.

■ Assessing your information needs realistically

Thirdly, few information sources are able to provide information that meets all the requirements for quality at a price that most of us can afford. Indeed, there's an equation around obtaining information that looks a bit like this:

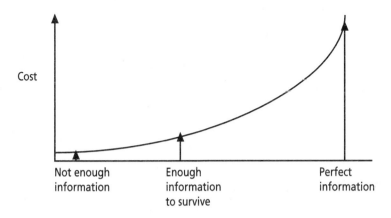

You need to continually reassess your information needs to make sure your sources give you enough to survive.

Sifting through the wealth of information

It's becoming easier to obtain information. But how does one manage the sheer wealth of it effectively? How can you recognize the information that really matters? How can you make sure you have the crucial point at your fingertips just when you need it?

Mike Hartley, writing in the *Coopers & Lybrand Bankers' Digest* of summer 1995, argues that the full potential of the "knowledge assets" of organizations is not being realized.

> In essence it is the conversion of information into knowledge which is often breaking down and limiting the potential of new information opportunities. Sorting through the information jungle and maximizing these opportunities is going to be increasingly

Mike Hartley,
*Coopers &
Lybrand Bankers'
Digest*

important as banks strive to get an edge on their competitors. The key question in the future will increasingly be not "what information?" but "who uses selective information to best effect?"

Hartley argues that "information in today's businesses only really enhances knowledge if it is selected, integrated with business processes and used effectively by people."

This to many is the nub of the information debate. We are "awash" with information. We face an information "deluge." We struggle to find the knowledge trees in the information "forest." We simply can't "absorb" the wealth of information around us.

It's worth unpacking this a little, as it hides a number of related problems.

The first problem is one of **aggregation** – of bringing information together and making meaning from it. We need ways of linking together information from different sources so that they add meaning to each other. At a basic level this has implications for activities such as filing – making sure that there is a clear system for storing and accessing information.

At a deeper level it involves being able to make connections, to see links and to recognize synergies.

The second problem is one of **selection** – of weeding out the less important information confidently. This happens at a number of stages. Crucial is receipt of information – unwanted, nonvaluable information must be rejected instantly, before it clogs up in-trays and databases. On a personal level this means creating the time to assess the value of information quickly.

The third problem is one of sharing – of communicating information to the people who need it.

The final problem is one of education – of ensuring that people know which information is important, why it is important, and what they can do with it.

Whatever way you look at the issue you do need to find a system for selecting the right information at the right time.

The new decision making

Taking decisions has always been a key part of the manager's role. But the changing nature of decision making has been one of the most fundamental shifts of the information age.

> Once it was possible to see decision making as an essentially rational process. Models were put forward of how you could take a good decision if you followed a series of logical steps.

Once it was possible to see decision making as an essentially rational process. Models were put forward of how you could take a good decision if you followed a series of logical steps.

Today, such models miss the fundamental point. Yes, you do need to bring logic and rationality to bear on your decisions. But you also – and this is crucial – need to bring creativity, flair, and intuition. And this makes the the manager's world increasingly scary and dangerous.

> Now a much higher proportion of decisions is unfamiliar. You have to think much harder before you take them. And you stand a higher chance of getting things wrong.

Why? Because before the information age more decisions were routine or repeat decisions. Many of the problems you faced were, in one way or another, familiar. You had applied solutions to similar problems before, and you could draw on this experience in taking the new decision.

Now a much higher proportion of decisions is unfamiliar. You have to think much harder before you take them. And you stand a higher chance of getting things wrong.

And yet it is ever more important to take decisions. As one chief executive said:

> "Many of the decisions I took were wrong. But the vital thing was that I took them."

So what can you do to become an effective decision-maker in the information age?

To start with, when taking any important decision it is now vital to consider a number of crucial factors:

- **Spoilt for choice.** There is likely to be a range of choices available to you – though they may not be immediately apparent. This means that you can't necessarily run with the first possible solution you think of. You need strategies for generating options, and in some cases these strategies need to be highly creative, imaginative, and original.

- **No right decision.** What's more, it's unlikely that any of these options will be the "right" decision. You are in the business of finding the best solution – or in some cases the least bad solution. Think for example of a senior management team confronted by a shortfall in sales. OK, it may be possible to find a way of getting sales back up to target. But you may be in the business of cutting costs, considering staff redundancies, job sharing, or part-time working. None of these is going to be an attractive option – but that makes it all the more important that you do generate as many options as possible, and select from them in a considered manner.

> When taking any important decision it is now vital to consider a number of crucial factors.

- **Multiple stakeholders.** On top of all this, important decisions are likely to affect a lot of people – your own team, colleagues, senior staff, customers, regulators, suppliers, the public. Each stakeholder will have their own interest in the outcome – and it's likely that these interests will conflict. Not only is there no right decision – what's best for one person may well upset someone else. All this makes decision making a highly political business, and today manager's decisions are under scrutiny more than ever before.

- **Under pressure.** Many managers must take big decisions fast, under high levels of pressure.

Secondly, you need to draw on a range of strategies to help you.

- **Know yourself** so you can learn to trust your intuition. Gut feel is an important part of decision making. But you need to know when you can trust gut feel, and when it may mislead you. As one of our colleagues commented:

  > "I don't really like formal meetings – I prefer less formal get togethers. But I know I have to be careful about this in planning projects. If I find myself thinking 'We don't need a meeting here' I have to ask myself 'Is this really true – or am I just trying to avoid something I don't like doing?'"

  Graham
  Willcocks,
  Wesley House

- **Generate options.** Creating options is possibly the most important part of the decision-making process. It involves being creative, and as such you need to be able to use creative techniques such as brainstorming or mind mapping. Group brainstorming can be one of the most effective ways of coming up with a range of options and gaining the benefit of several people's experience.

- **Apply criteria.** If generating options is the creative, lateral, right-brain activity, then applying criteria is the analytical, left-brain side of the equation. You need a mechanism for comparing options and making as rational as possible a choice between them. To do this you need to identify the key criteria that a decision must satisfy. You can consider weighting them if some are more important than others.

- **Assess stakeholder interests.** We don't take decisions in a vacuum. Important decisions will affect other key stakeholders. It's important to consider these implications in the process of selecting from the options available.

- **Develop team decision making.** As self-managing teams become more important, so they need to develop the skills of decision making as well.

- **Face up to tough decisions.** Just because teams can make decisions doesn't mean that you can abdicate responsibility.

Managers have to be able to decide, especially in those difficult no-win situations.

- **Follow decisions through.** Finally, remember that taking a decision is just a start. Equally important is the process of selling and implementing it.

■ Living with fallibility

The harder the choices you face, the more often you will make decisions that go down badly and may be "wrong." There's no point in pretending that this is not the case – but it's vital to be able to live with the consequences.

> The first key thing here is that you need a culture that doesn't blame people for making mistakes. And you can contribute to this by not blaming other people for making poor decisions, but by helping them to tackle the problems.

The first key thing here is that you need a culture that doesn't blame people for making mistakes. And you can contribute to this by not blaming other people for making poor decisions, but by helping them to tackle the problems.

It's vital also to reflect on your own decisions and to learn from them, good or bad. It also helps if you can admit that you have made a mistake yourself. Many decisions are not final – there is scope to modify or change them later. The worst thing is to pretend nothing is wrong while everything is falling down around you.

Communicating information effectively

Decision making is one key way of using information. Another vital use of information is communication. And the information champion must be a champion for information sharing, exchange, and communication. This in turn makes them champions of people who need information – be they people elsewhere in the organization, or people in the wider world like customers and consumers.

This involves turning the quality information checklist the other way round. It involves asking ourselves what information people need, when and where they need it, and in what form or medium.

Mike Bartram from Consumer Congress tells us:

> "Public services in particular need to be educated about how people use information. Most consumers get most of what they need to know by talking to people and watching the telly. Yet for years too many managers have failed to grasp this apparently obvious fact, bombarding us with glossy leaflets and requiring complainants to write in if they want redress. This hardly inspires confidence that the managers will understand the possibilities and limitations of the developing technology."

Mike Bartram,
Consumer
Congress

The information champion needs especially to use new media effectively. He or she is able to use the right media at the right time – be it Intranet, Internet, CD ROM or the humble old, and often ignored, letter or telephone call.

The key to selecting the right media is to think about the receiver of the message. It's no good going high tech if high tech won't work.

So there should be a process:

1 *What do you want to say?*

2 *Who are you saying it to?*

3 *How would the receiver like to receive the message?*

But championing the information user also involves a new mind set, one that subversively asks why – why do we keep this information from people? Why don't we ask people what information they need? Why don't we share information more widely?

Championing learning

There's no doubt that information champions will also be a champions for learning. This has several implications. They will learn constantly themselves. They will be good at helping others to learn.

■ Learning constantly

We have a colleague who asks himself at the end of every day: "What have I learned today?"

How do we become effective learners? There are several tools available – try them out and use those that suit you. To start with, there are tools for reflecting on your experience and learning from it:

Learning logs

A learning log is a record of any significant experience, together with your reflection on what you learned from it. It can be a sheet of paper, a page in a filofax, a note on the PC. It's likely to include a date, a description of what happened, a summary of what you learned, and a note of what you intend to do as a result.

Portfolios

Increasingly, information champions are building portfolios of their achievements. A portfolio can contain achievements from any part of your life. Cross-referencing portfolios can help you see the links and create new synergies.

There are also tools for learning by doing, by trying things out in practice. These include:

Experiments

Scientists have always used experiments as a way of learning.

Donald Schön – who we'll meet again in chapter eight – argues that professionals do this as well.

According to Schön, effective practitioners deal with new and unfamiliar problems by constructing an experiment. They entertain a number of hypotheses that may explain the problem facing them. They test out the hypotheses by trying them out and seeing what happens. In doing this they interact with the problem and may well change it.

We come back to this theme in chapter eight.

■ Helping others to learn

Not only will the information champion be good at learning – he or she will be good at helping others to learn as well. The information champion will accept as part of his or her day-to-day work the need to coach and mentor other people in the organization.

> Coaching is face-to-face leadership that pulls together people with diverse backgrounds, talents, experiences, and interests, encourages them to step up to responsibility and continued achievement. Coaching is not about memorizing techniques or devising the perfect game plan. It is also about really paying attention to people, really involving them.

Tom Peters and Robert Waterman, *In search of Excellence*

The skilled coach is able to do a number of interesting balancing acts:

- They balance direction with self-management. They can help their protégé to identify useful opportunities for learning. They are able to negotiate and agree targets for learning. They agree ways and means of monitoring progress.

- They balance a range of learning methods – they know when it's best to tell or show someone how to do something, and when it's better for them to try something out for themselves with support.

- They balance giving people autonomy and responsibility with making sure that they have support and don't go off the rails in a destructive way. They do this by defining tasks clearly, setting clear limits to responsibility and agreeing review points.

● They balance consistency with creativity.

Networking skills

Mel Velarde, General Manager of Philippine TV company Sky Cable, Quoted in 'How IT is changing the way you manage', in *World's Executive Digest Technology,* September 1995.

A modern chief executive running a high-risk, fast-paced company can no longer sit in his office and require people to make appointments before they can see him. Though I have organized self-directed teams in clusters and encourage decision-making by people in the field, I want to be accessible to everyone. Technology helps me. A boss has to be on-line. I can listen and talk to employees in all departments.

In many ways networking can been seen as putting up a receiver to the world. Despite all the data warehouses, Internets, Intranets, and the like, sometimes the very best way to find information is to be in touch with people and the ideas they have.

Networking is a highly valued advanced-level information-age skill for the following reasons.

● You just hear things – facts, figures, gossip, market intelligence. All can be useful.
● You stay in touch with people who can keep you abreast of new technological developments. As we have seen the world is changing fast and getting out of the office and talking to people can help you to keep abreast.
● It keeps you sane – with all the information buzzing around, just meeting people and sharing an insight into their and your world can be a valuable stress reliever and reality check.
● It can help you to gain influence.

Networking must happen at several levels. It happens within the organization. As an internal HR consultant in one organization told us:

> "The new technologies – in particular voice mail and e-mail – are invaluable in my work. But they are no substitute for face-to-face networking. If I come out of a meeting and find a message on my voice mail, I often try to return it in person, 'by hand' if you like. It shows people I'm available. It helps me extend my network and build my contacts. It keeps me in touch and lets me know what's going on."

It also happens between organizations, and this is where the role of the boundary worker is so critical. Boundary workers need to be able to exchange information effectively with partner organizations.

> Despite all the data warehouses, Internets, Intranets, and the like, sometimes the very best way to find information is to be in touch with people and the ideas they have.

Networking is also vital for the growing number of people outside the conventional organization – consultants, small teams of associates, little organizations supplying the big ones. Two of our colleagues have set up a series of "learning lunches" for people doing similar work to them in their locality. On a regular basis a group of consultants and freelancers get together over lunch to share ideas, exchange information, and learn from each other.

■ Cooperative self-sufficiency

Networking brings into sharp focus the need for co-operative self-sufficiency – the need to be an effective member of the self-managing team.

Information champions need to be self-reliant. They need to be able to work alone, to take tough decisions, to go out on a limb, to interact with the technology.

But they also need to get along with other people well. They need to be able to show respect and demonstrate that they value others.

This is why the propellor heads really are the wrong people for the job, as we argued in chapter two. The information champions come out from behind the VDU, leave behind the darkened rooms and get a life.

Another letter from the information age

This letter comes from Saj Arshad of Visa International. He explains his own journey to information champion. It is interesting because it shows a mix of predisposition and skills building as key elements in the armory of any information champion.

It also paints a vivid picture of the way organizations are responding to the change.

What is the information age?

The Information age exists, but I think we need to step outside the technology view. Technology is merely the enabler that allows us to manipulate data.

What's interesting, is that the information age is about allowing ordinary people access to a global pool of data and what this means is that we're moving back to a kind of cottage industry.

In other words, in the old cottage industry days companies knew their customers almost one to one. The aim today is to get back to that situation - we should be able to know our customers intimately and service their needs in a precise fashion. It's the information age that is increasingly allowing us to do this.

It's true that technology allows you to manipulate data in a meaningful way and really get to know consumers, but there really is so much of it about.

Ideally you want to capture data on every transaction a customer makes, because then you can package up a real profile of that individual and then target goods and services toward them.

Don't get carried away by the technology

Every invention has been a new technology. If you think about it, fire was a technology, electricity was a technology. Technology in and of itself is not a new thing. All inventions do is to refine our ability to handle larger and larger volumes of data. And this is important in an increasingly complex world. This is all this next phase of technology is. It just allows nontechnical experts to manipulate large quantities of data in a better and a more efficient way. This is fundamentally what the revolution is about.

What's happened with a lot of the technology is that it gets easier to use. Take, for instance, the PC or mainframe. They start off very difficult to use and very expert oriented. Over time as the use grows they become more democratised. The interfaces are built to become easier and this will continue. So a lot of the fear currently about technology is likely to dissolve over the years.

Turbo charged professionals

At the moment this ability to deal with the simple interfaces is just the basic entry point. The real stars are going to need slightly different sets of skills. They'll need to go beyond an appreciation of how to use something as basic as "Windows." They'll need to become adept at manipulating the technology to serve their needs.

In a sense, though, people do need a predisposition to using the technology.

They don't need to be technophiles. They do need to be excited by the technology and go beyond the basics. They take on board the technology and are inquisitive about it.

My own interest comes from a long-standing interest in science fiction.

Things that are happening now I read about as a child and so I'm not frightened but fascinated by it. I think this interest in the technology is the key.

It's not important to share the same background as me, but the type of person that will succeed needs to be at ease with technology and understand that it's a means to an end and not an end in itself. They can then manipulate it to suit them and make the necessary leaps that each successive technology brings. It's about constant learning.

Information and knowledge

What we really need is to create the learning organisation. This is all the more important given the sheer volume of information that's actually available to organisations these days. But the challenge we face is even more basic than this.

Visa is good at dealing with information but even so we still face a deluge of the stuff. We have a huge well of data that is only kept for a certain period. We need to use this information as effectively as possible. The real issue is how to turn that information into knowledge.

So what do we do? How do we learn, how do we keep that knowledge in the company and share it among ourselves? The way we do it is partly through our culture. It's through the people skills that are often undervalued in this information age. People tend to stay at Visa a long time – because they like working here, because it's a challenge and because they feel welcome within the culture. They have the freedom to move round within the company which means they can share their expertise and knowledge.

So in addition to having systems and processes that capture the knowledge in the organisation and share it (on an Intranet), we go for a very simple idea that is if you keep people working for you and they're happy then that information and knowledge is always available.

We haven't got an expert system to capture the knowledge. However, we do have a neural network system that is programmed with basic knowledge. It learns as it goes on. It's continually updated. This neural network analyses cardholder spending. It can basically tell whether a card is possibly being used fraudulently by analysing cardholders' past spending habits and the way the card is being used now. In other words, people pour their expertise into the system and the system then learns and grows.

So we are starting to act as a knowledge and learning organization.

But there's also an argument for operating the other way. Not filtering out bad transactions but looking for good transactions. If we can find out that people for instance shop twice a week at a particular store then we can start to actually put together offers that will appeal to those people.

What does an information revolution boil down to?

For me as a marketer, the information revolution has greatly enhanced my ability to deliver ever more sophisticated products and services, to ever smaller segments, whilst adding ever greater value to that relationship. And I think it's the new tools and techniques that will allow all organisations to become much more customer focused. It will help us to be more responsive and flexible.

How have things changed?

Superficially my job is pretty much the same as it was five years ago. At a deeper level there are major differences.

Five years ago I was sitting at a desk having lots of meetings with clients, suppliers and internal customers and working occasionally on a PC. I still do all of those things but there have been real changes.

What we have come to realise is that simply working at a distance isn't the answer to everything. Sure, people could work out of the office a lot of the time, but the more time you spend away from customers *and away from the team here, the less creative you are. The more separated you are from the building itself and for us, that really wouldn't be a good thing.*

Everyone could work from home with their PCs and modems The infrastructure exists. However, in this type of marketing team, it just doesn't work. You need the sparking off each other. Many teams just couldn't work unless everyone was hot housed in this office. So five years on I think we'll still be doing that. I think we'll still be working together as a team. I don't think we'll all be working from home.

But there are real other changes. There has been a productivity gain. But this has obviously come at a cost. It's cost a great deal of money to equip me with a computer and other infrastructure.

Some of the mundane tasks have become easier which has freed me up. But I've had to learn a far wider range of skills and this business of continually learning is the new paradigm. I think in five years' time that the need to learn and learn quickly will be even more important.

Once upon a time you were just the marketing manager, but now you need to be a good project manager, finance manager, a salesman, a general manager, a person manager – something marketers have traditionally been poor at, a good leader and motivator.

What's interesting is that the information age has actually focused us much more on developing a whole range of personal skills. And we can do that because our time has been really freed up by the information revolution, and it's filled up, not with menial work anymore but with real people and other skills.

So the manager of the future is really going to be a knowledge manager. They certainly won't fit into traditional roles.

Let's look at e-mail. It certainly leads to a significant time saving and I certainly would never like to be without it again. It is a help. It's great for scheduling meetings and so on. There is a significant time saving here. I can check people's diaries much more easily. There's less fiddling about. And this is one of the significant differences from five years ago. Because there's a PC on every desktop at Visa now, it'll be unheard of for most managers to give their secretaries a letter or memo to type. We do all these things ourselves and use assistants for higher value projects.

And the whole time this ability is being upgraded. These days I do my own spreadsheets, faxes, letters and presentation. I can also schedule meetings through my machines and so on.

So these things have all helped incrementally. However, what's happened is other things fill the time. For a start, my day has got longer and I think this will continue. I think that's what's happening is there's more and more emphasis being put on us being multi-skilled and it's the technology, the information revolution that's actually facilitated this.

Because you have to be a master of all trades there is a tremendous fragmentation of the working day. We have our electronic diary which divides our day up hour to hour. This means we don't really have time to sit down and really concentrate on one task. We have become facilitators because the electronic diary has in many ways made us be so. When your day is broken up into countless small blocks you need to then spend time managing others. What also happens is that in this new information age the survivors will be able to flit from task to task. They will need to be very very adaptable and in this environment you survive by being able to do a lot of different things at the same time.

In any given day I'll do five or six completely different things or completely unrelated projects. And that's the norm. The fragmentation of the day is a real feature of the information revolution.

After the wave front of any new technology the regular people move in. And my view is it's the regular people with added-value skills that will inherit the earth in terms of the way the revolution is going. I've got absolutely no doubt about it.

Technology drives itself forward

Often it is technology directors who drive the developments. However, there's no-one now saying that despite all the money we've spent that we have enough to do what we need. You still see some very large organizations making questionable IT investments that cost simply millions of dollars. And I think in a way one of the problems we have is that there may become a time when the sheer investment does not really make a return. The spending is huge on this information age and we shouldn't underestimate it. Who is measuring the rate of return or the productivity?

But always organizations need to ask themselves whether they're really getting benefit out of it. There is something about the fact that people really do just want to be seen to be doing the right thing, and I don't think that's a way to carry the revolution forward.

There is a great deal we can take from the letter above. For instance, that information champions need a mix of predisposition and application. We also get a view of the way the nature of work is changing, and all either driven or facilitated by the information revolution. We can also see that information champions are dedicated to learning and helping their colleagues to learn.

But in our final postcard from the information in this section Jane Greene a writer adds an interesting dimension to the debate.

The new employee and the new organisation

I believe the information age will be hugely important. It will increase the speed information travels and consequently the whole world will speed up. On the positive side I believe it will open up information. Companies and governments will not be able to keep the lid on information. We will have more of an information democracy.

> *As far as managers go there are a whole range of things managers will need just to gain entry to the new age. They need to be able to judge what information is useful. There will be, and indeed is, so much information around they will not be able to read everything. So they will need the skills of quickly assessing information, grouping it, storing it and accessing it. In many ways they need to lose the idea that they need to read everything that comes across their desk. So they need to live in a contingent world.*
>
> *What is interesting is that the company of the future needs the same set of skills as the individual. Like individuals, companies will be faced with a wealth of information. They need to be aware of it but to be selective. They will use modems and the Internet and the like but will need really good information systems to make sure they use the information wisely.*

Jane Greene highlights a fundamental truth about the new age:

Managers and organizations need analogous skills – that the personal and the organizational are in the same boat.

And it is here that we can see that the people in organizations and the organizations themselves need to develop organically in terms of skills. Jane Greene again:

> We can see the issue of skills sets – both for individuals and organizations in terms of CD ROMs. CD ROMs are the living embodiment of the information age. Where before you had a book-based encyclopaedia, it now fits onto a tiny disk. This is amazing. But whether a CD ROM actually works depends on how well the information is structured and the retrieval mechanism. If the navigation is poor a CD ROM is just so much data – useless and unused. In the same way managers and organizations need make sure they can retrieve information effectively.

References

Bartram, M. *Consumer Congress Newsletter,* Summer 1996.

Hartley, M. *Coopers & Lybrand Bankers Digest*, Summer 1995.

Peters, T. and Waterman, W. *In Search of Excellence*, Harper Collins, 1989.

Schön, D. *The Reflective Practitioner: How Professionals Think in Action*, Basic Books, 1983.

"How IT is changing the way you manage," in *World's Executive Digest Technology*, September 1995.

chapter seven

CREATING ORGANIZATIONS FIT FOR AN INFORMATION REVOLUTION

- They come in all shapes and sizes
- Some organizational paradigms

We have invented a range of different organizational paradigms with the aim of exploring which kind of organization is likely to survive and thrive

This and the following two sections look at the organizational perspective. They look at how organizations can adapt in order to make the most of the possibilities afforded by the information age.

In this chapter, though, we have some fun.

We have invented a range of different organizational paradigms with the aim of exploring which kind of organization is likely to survive and thrive.

They come in all shapes and sizes

The organization of the information age with be of it and in it. It will not be a distant and bemused spectator in proceedings. It will grasp the new challenges with gusto, live with inconsistency and look to reinvent itself when needed. Old money and privilege are likely to be given scant regard in the new age.

And so the info-organization will come in all shapes and sizes – big, small, fat, and thin.

The successful organization may consist of someone sitting in a shed on a hilltop connected to the world via 'phone, modems, and the like, and running a completely virtual organization. It may consist of a sparkly, extensive, and expensive head office with literally thousands of employees. One successful information organization we have heard of consists of one person operating four Apple Macs at the same time!

What will matter will be the organization's attitude to information, its responsiveness, its willingness to stay open to information and not be crushed by the weight of it, or the lure of it. What is certain is that information – using it, gaining it, passing it on to customers, incorporating it in products and services – is likely to be at the core of the business. And new technology is bound to play a major part, whatever the business you are in.

So the only rule may be that there are no rules. And the shape of the organizations that result will be highly unpredictable.

The following range of organizational types operates along a continuum. The first organizational type is the one we feel is least satisfactory, the last the most – although circumstances will differ, and you may find that all of them have a role to play at different times.

Some organizational paradigms

So here we go. Which of the following most resembles your place of work? If it's the first, you have our commiserations and maybe you should look for a new job.

■ 1 The poisoned library

In the film version of Umberto Eco's marvellous book *The Name of Rose*, Sean Connery plays a Benedictine monk who becomes involved in an epic murder mystery.

The Connery figure arrives for an ecumenical conference at a somewhat sinister abbey. It quickly becomes clear that something is very wrong. A string of deaths takes place, each victim a monk, each monk found with blackened tongue, poisoned, and decidedly dead.

Connery takes up the challenge of investigating and eventually discovers the abbey's gruesome secret. The abbey contains a secret library, containing all the books with forbidden knowledge (notably Aristotle's treatise on laughter). But humans are humans, and monks are fond of a good laugh. So the dead monks had all been tempted by the forbidden knowledge; they gained access to the library and turned the pages in order to read. Sadly for them, the pages were poisoned so as deter such behavior.

The film may be one of the greatest shaggy dog stories of all time, but it does strike a chord.

Many organizations view knowledge in this way. It is guarded, dangerous, and kept locked away. Only certain elders are allowed access to it and those who attempt to find out more are punished (although not usually by poisoning!). Many organizations create the unnatural silence and calm of the abbey library.

These organizations are kind of walled gardens to the world. They operate using strict and frankly bizarre rules and regulations. They are based on secrecy for its own sake. They attempt to shut out and control information. For them the contingent universe is simply an annoyance and so they go about ignoring its existence. Information and knowledge are poison and staff must be kept in the dark. Only those of rank and influence have access to it. And so these organizations are divorced from the world. They do not grow. They are stuck in a moment in time.

> Because of the speed that information travels these days, this means that you cannot hold the hands of the clock still.

And here there is an interesting, not to say profound, point. Because of the speed that information travels these days, this means that you cannot hold the hands of the clock still. When a single credit card transaction can speed through computer and telephone lines around the world in five seconds then we are virtually in a world of time travel. So building a wall and hoping the world will go away isn't an option.

There are, though, still many many organizations like this. Believe us, we have worked for some of them. But this kind of approach at an organizational level is doomed to failure (as it was in *The Name of the Rose*). Today, in the world as it is, the walls have come down and you cannot shut out the world. And dangerous ideas, information and knowledge are let loose.

And in organizational terms, the poisoned library has other things to teach us. In the film, the poison library has a single keeper. He guards the knowledge in the library ferociously. When an intruder (Sean Connery) gains access to the inner sanctum of the library, the keeper sets fire to the library rather than see the secrets shared. There is an implosion and the whole abbey burns. In today's environment, trying to keep out the world and unnaturally restrict information flows is just like putting a match to the company itself.

■ 2 The watchtower approach

Some organizations have moved away from the poisoned library – just. The approach resembles that of a watchtower.

Let's take you back a few centuries to when there were castles. In those days you built a castle – normally to keep out invaders and on a nearby hill you placed a watchtower.

> Many organizations take a watchtower approach. They establish a data-gathering department, leave it all to them and then get on with their "real" work.

The idea was that the soldiers on the watchtower took responsibility for keeping an eye on what was happening in the world. When there was a problem they let you know by building a bonfire. The serene calm in the castle was then disturbed by a frantic pulling up of the portcullis and general making ready for confrontation. Unless the bonfire was lit the castle paid no attention to the rest of the world. It handed the responsibility for information to a small elite guard and relied completely on that.

This had some advantages. For the people inside the castle they could feel confident that they were safe. For those in the watchtower it meant great prestige and power.

But the problem came when the watchtower soldiers were caught asleep, or outmanuvered as an enemy approached. If they were looking the wrong way, disaster followed. And anyway you can never cram enough eyes and ears into a watchtower to really cover all the bases.

So let's look at some organizational analogies again. Many organizations take a watchtower approach. They establish a data-gathering department, leave it all to them and then get on with their "real" work.

But in today's world this is as doomed to failure as the poisoned library. For a start it takes responsibility for gathering and using information away from the vast bulk of employees. Their information skills decline or never grow and they lose any understanding of just how important it is for all staff to take part in the information age. They cease to be the army of information champions that any organization needs to survive and thrive.

> The systems start to drive the business. If they say they can't process something for six months because the computer won't let them, what can you do? The tail wags the dog and the customer perspective gets lost.

And then those in the data department get too powerful. The systems start to drive the business. If they say they can't process something for six months because the computer won't let them, what can you do? The tail wags the dog and the customer perspective gets lost. You get a benign technical dictatorship breaking out and the organization starts to suffer. The digerati gain undue power to the detriment of the organization itself.

And while they are meant to be looking outward from the watchtower, they start fiddling around with the computer systems and you find all the good people have been re-engineered out of a job. It happens.

And what if they get it wrong? What if they get outflanked by a new threat, challenge or opportunity? You're sunk. The watchtower contingent was asleep or looking the wrong way.

While your data department was looking the other way, some other up-and-coming bunch stole all your business.

So, you'll gather that we don't recommend the watchtower approach. We don't because we believe that the world has become too fast, too complex, too exciting to leave all the watching to a chosen few.

In our ideal model an organization should work to empower everyone to gain information skills and use them – not just the chosen few.

■ 3 The digital hive

This model is plain scary. Its implications have been explained in their most apocalyptic form in a book called *War of the Worlds* by Mark Slouka who teaches at the University of California.

In an article in *The Guardian*, Slouka explains a nightmare scenario where people will soon have wired themselves together with the new technology to such an extent that they won't be individuals anymore. All information will be added to the collective mind – the Net.

People may simply become drones – governed by the hive. And this according to some is the next stage in human evolution. It could be driven by huge databases and would certainly spell the end of work as we know it.

Obviously there is the whiff of sci-fi about this but the notion of the organization as hive has been taken up by some. Slouka eloquently points to the danger inherent in the loss of individualism which would come about as a result of organization as digital hive.

The reason why this mechanistic approach won't work is that it is people's individuality and inspirations that will really help make the most of the information age. As we have said many times in the book it is people skills that will be every bit as important as technology skills in the information age.

The problem with the digital hive is that it takes away the individual's power to take decisions. It is role dominated and thrives on demarcation.

In a hive everyone is a strict functional specialist. Everyone contributes something – but only a small something. Gone is the idea of the all-rounder (incidentally an idea that David Wynne-Owen explained so eloquently in the last chapter). In fact, we believe the success stories of the future will be genuine all-rounders – with technical and people skills.

In the hive you have no Renaissance individuals – just a series of people forced to act in role for the greater good. Not nice.

■ 4 The mesh

Another model for the information age is the mesh. Where the hive is role dominated, the mesh is technology dominated.

In the mesh all information is filtered to a complex, technologically advanced system based on new telecommunications. Each part of the system is dependent on other parts of the system. It deals in a standard way with large volumes (and incidentally is excellent for this purpose).

Such a system relies on rapid switching of information into available channels. It relies on fast response times, through power dialing systems and databases.

The customer rings from anywhere in the world and gets through immediately to the organization. The organization then deals with any requests in the blink of an eye. Within moments, the product or service is sold and the paperwork processed.

This system works particularly well when the company is selling simple and standard products and operates through a high-tech interdependent system.

It is highly reliant on technology and staff are there to operate the equipment and process calls or other information. In many ways it is an advanced information factory.

It can work and the lure of such an approach is obvious. After all wouldn't it be marvelous to set up a system that took the doubt out of the world?

Why not offer a quick reliable system that is of the moment and which ties up all the loose ends neatly?

But the problem with the mesh as a model is that:

- It tends to downgrade the role of people;
- If the technology crashes you cannot operate;
- It is slow to change because of the reliance on the system and is very expensive to set up and maintain;
- It works less well with complex products, services, and situations.

The mesh is good when dealing with a large volume of similar transactions. It is efficient and can offer the values of speed and conformity. But there are risks associated with it – especially when used inappropriately. And maybe, the mesh is just a little colorless in terms of the people and the resultant customer loyalty. As an entity the mesh does not learn or grow – it is constrained by the technology, at least at the moment.

One thing our work with organizations in the information age shows us is that panaceas and quick fixes and miracle cures don't work. Salesmen like to tell you they work, but they don't really.

■ 5 The Jesuit college

In sixteenth and seventeenth century Spain and Portugal the Jesuits developed a model of a learning organization that has continued virtually to this day – and especially in the context of the information revolution.

In the Jesuit system, the priests were all given identical training. The movement itself valued learning highly and believed the priests should be of the world and in the world.

Having been trained, the priests would leave the college and then go out into the community. They would teach their particular form of Catholicism with its own emphasis on challenging orthodoxies and the pursuit of knowledge as well as belief.

After a time, the priests would return to the college that they trained in and bring back what they had learned. This learning was then assimilated and the college would adjust the way it taught new priests.

It is and was an interesting model. The Jesuits founded many of the ancient universities in Europe. They understood that learning was important and being in the world was important and that organizations grow as a result of the knowledge. They challenged the way the world was. The priest was an all-rounder – a holy man, a scholar, a learner, and a listener.

But there are still drawbacks in this model in organizational terms. Although they had an inquiring disposition they still had their own religious doctrines and dogmas that limited their capacity to learn. In today's new revolution, a dogma may be disastrous. And in the longer run the Jesuits were persecuted by the state and mother church because they didn't stick close to the center.

> After a time, the priests would return to the college that they trained in and bring back what they had learned. This learning was then assimilated and the college would adjust the way it taught new priests.

■ 6 The lighthouse approach

This is an interesting one and has many virtues. If you've ever been lost at sea in a force niner then a lighthouse would make a very welcome sight indeed.

The lighthouse is basically simple. It is static and sends out the same information all the time (via a flashing light). The information itself is unambiguous but useful, not to say vital. The lighthouse broadcasts information, but does not receive it.

You can see the lighthouse model in organizational terms. Many organizations send out information which is useful. However, they see information in one-dimensional terms – as a broadcast

> Internet forums, complaints schemes, focus groups, market intelligence bulletins, market research, and the like are all part of the two-way dialogue organizations need.

medium. This kind of organization may produce excellent brochures and other communications, but it does not get real feedback in from customers or information from the world at large.

In today's environment, the whole business of communications has become interactive. You talk to the world; the world talks to you. Just look at the opportunities for two-way dialogue and information gathering that exist.

Internet forums, complaints schemes, focus groups, market intelligence bulletins, market research, and the like are all part of the two-way dialogue organizations need.

If you are stuck sending out the same message and not receiving messages in return, then you are taking part in only half the story.

The lighthouse works in a limited way, but in organizational terms is a wasted opportunity. And look at the problems associated with not listening.

New Coke

A few years ago Coca Cola in the USA decided that it had to make some changes. It was spending more than $100 million dollars more than Pepsi on advertising and yet was losing market share. It decided to replace the existing product with New Coke and launch it as a replacement product. It carried out trials of the new product taste and found that people liked it, and so forged ahead.

But Coca Cola admits now that it failed to ask a fairly fundamental question: "How will people feel if the old product isn't available any more?" Mind you, Coke is just a soft drink so it's not really a question of feelings or emotions, is it? Well, yes, as it turned out. The whole story is about emotions and tradition, rather than the taste of a soft drink.

Within three days of the switch to New Coke, the company was receiving 8,000 calls of complaint a day. Acquaintances and passers-by in supermarkets and on the street abused Coca Cola executives, and some were even threatened with death. There were letters saying things like:

"You have personally stolen something from me. ... it's mine and I want it back."

"You have betrayed me and the American way of life."

A black market trade started, with franchized bottling plants making and selling "bootleg" old coke at three times the price. Illegal imports of the old product came in from Mexico and other countries. Coke trucks containing the old product were hijacked and the contents sold. Frank Olsen and Gary Milkins, in Seattle, started an organization called *The Old Cola Drinkers of America*. They set up a full-time office and became hugely popular guests on TV talk shows. They said "It's *my* drink. ... it's part of our country." They even went as far as suing Coca Cola in an unsuccessful attempt to get the old product reinstated.

For most of this time, Coca Cola executives seemed to be shutting their eyes and ears to the outcry. They didn't quite know what to do, but to the outside world it felt as if the company was doing what it wanted to do rather than listen to the customers. But they also had to take account of the fact that thousands of people apparently did like New Coke. They weren't saying much, but they were buying the product,

Something had to be done. The choices were to revert to the original position, stick to the new one, or find some sort of middle way. Eventually, the chief executive announced that it was responding to public pressure. Original Coca Cola was reborn as Classic Coke.

The whole experience took everyone by surprise.

Quoted from *Connecting with Customers*, by S. Morris and G. Willcocks.

■ 7 The trading post

And now one of many favored models – the trading post.

It has been said that there are too many cowboys involved in the new technology world. But remember it was the cowboys who won the wild west. And in many ways the environment is like the wild west. Why? Well:

- There is a vast number of people wanting a piece of the action;
- It is rough and tough, not to say cut-throat;
- It is virgin territory;
- Cultures are clashing.

And there is an organizational "Boot Hill." Just look at the number of old-established companies disappearing from the Fortune 500 index.

Perhaps one of the most satisfactory organization in today's information age would resemble the trading post. The trading post was open to all. It sustained the west. In the community of the trading post there is room for old and young and a variety of different skills and attributes. It can be a balanced community (in the way we recommend that organizations themselves need to maintain balanced communities).

What binds the parties together is trade and mutual advantage and support. The trading post can exist in the most hostile terrain. It can be staffed by an individual or by an army of different people.

The trading post is firmly fixed in the world. It is not distanced from it. It relies on understanding the world about it and anticipating its needs. It is a provider and a processor, and it is pragmatic. If you need to operate with a computerized system, then operate through one. If pen and paper will do, then pen and paper it is.

And the modern organization will be trading on information –

- Using it to add value;
- Accessing it from where it can;
- Using it in ways that suits the customer; and
- Prepared to change whenever needed.

Anyone who has traveled will know that trading posts can be found in the most amazing places. In a jungle or in a high-tech metropolis. And so it is with our modern organization. It is flexible enough to be where the trade is – and that might be in a hut on a hillside or in the central business district of London or New York.

> We believe that there are real parallels between the workings of the human brain and the information-age company.

And the information trading post handles an intangible product – information that it can turn to tangible benefits. It might be a simple and single cell, or joined by telecoms to all parts of the globe.

■ 8 Developing the corporate brain

This is the final model – and one that finds favor with us too. We believe that there are real parallels between the workings of the human brain and the information-age company. Let's start with the brain.

The brain is a tremendous thing. It is made up of neurones. Each neurone is a tiny cell. Each neurone is genetically identical to every other cell. All neurones are interconnected. The cells in the brain are connected to each other by tendrils.

If a cell is stimulated it will resonate with all the cells around it. Each holds different memories. Some seem immediately relevant, others not. When a cell is stimulated, it triggers off the possibility of hundreds of chance encounters with other cells.

The brain renews itself. It does have uncharted areas that don't seem to do much. These are likely to be spare capacity that we can fill when needed. Incidentally, people who suffer brain damage in a stroke are helped to activate some of these dormant areas.

And the way the brain handles information is a true piece of magic. The brain (like the modern organization) handles a vast amount of information and stimuli. There is the information from the five senses all the time and usually simultaneously. There is also the internal information – for instance the brain tells the heart to beat each second or so.

But the brain can handle it – and handle it at once. It does two things. It establishes a hierarchy of information. If you pick up a boiling plate from the oven by mistake it prioritizes the information from the senses – this hurts – and does something about it. You drop the plate. But as well as establishing a hierarchy, it also has the capacity for brilliant pieces of lateral thinking as the neurones resonate with each other. So the brain is pragmatic and has values.

But how can we see the organization of the information age in these terms?

Well:

- It also needs to be fiercely interconnected. The information that comes in needs to resonate and create ideas and inspirations within different departments (unlike in the poisoned library where information is cut off);
- It needs to be open to internal and external stimuli;
- It also needs to establish a hierarchy of information when needed;
- It needs values;
- It needs all-rounders within it, similar to the way neurones are;
- It needs to have the capacity to grow and learn;
- It needs to be geared toward action;
- It needs spare information storage capacity that it can grow into;
- It needs to have a magic combination of machine and inspiration and emotion and memory.

And as with the brain, it is not a free-for-all. The brain is organic and highly organized. It is responsive. It is a machine, but it is what makes us human.

But how to get there? And how to get there especially if you are working in an organization with an unsatisfactory model? Well, it will take great leadership and probably restructuring. But it should be within reach. After all, it is natural. Every worker in an organization has a brain that works in this self-same way. We need to plug back in to what we already know.

And a final thought on the brain. It is said that humans learn the most in the first four years of life. If we kept learning at this rate, we would be a formidable and amazing species. But we stop — maybe we get tired out with the effort of it all. But in organizational terms what we may need is childish organizations. Ones that can accelerate through those early years and learn and keep on learning.

And finally

So these are just some ideas about the shape and feel of the information-age organization. What it shows is that the old ways of constructing organizations is likely to have to go. And we say, "*good riddance.*"

What it also shows is that the organizational map of the future is likely to be different. We are seeing it already, with the growth of small virtual organizations. Perhaps a personal postcard from the information age will show the flavour of the new reality.

The Burton Morris Consultancy

We offer a writing service to organisations in the public and private sector. This includes writing material into plain English and other copywriting. The company also produces materials on management and organizations.

It is a virtual organization in a number of key respects. First, it has a small number of core staff – three at the company's office. Second, it contracts teams of people to work on projects as and when they are needed – end of project, end of contract. Third, these teams are spread around the UK and are made up of specialist writers and designers. Fourth, these teams are linked up by telecoms: everyone works on a MAC, each has a modem and fax machine, each stays in regular touch by 'phone – meetings are kept to an absolute minimum.

To the client, the joins don't show. Although the client knows the BMC team is dispersed and brought together for the project it feels cohesive, with each team member sharing the same set of values and commitment to doing things The Burton Morris way. A virtual organisation must actually feel like a real organisation to the customer – a flesh and blood group of people pulling together with a focal point that takes responsibility.

This is how it worked on a recent project. TSB contracted BMC to redraft 150 customer letters into plain English. BMC put a team together to complete the job – a specialist full-time plain English writer, an editor and proof reader, a legal specialist to check for legal accuracy and a project manager to liaise with the client and make sure the project moved though on time. The project manager worked at BMC's office, the rest worked from home. The director of BMC and the project manager met the client and agreed exact requirements. They briefed other members of the team. The writer wrote the new letters and modemed text through to BMC, the director read and suggested changes, the lawyer checked for legal issues, the writer made the changes and the proof reader checked the results.

> *Three weeks later the client received 150 letters, produced internally by the BMC team. At this stage the writer and lawyer had finished their work. The client sent through revisions, the project manager hired an inputter to input the text, the proof reader checked them and the director read them all through before they were sent off. One happy client, one no-hassle job for them. Goodbye team, hello new team for the next job.*
>
> *The odd thing is that some of my closest friends and colleagues I speak to just over the 'phone. One of my key writers and close friends I talk to most days about our projects and the work we are doing together … and we never meet in person. Virtual organisations breed virtual friendships, and to my mind these are far better than the rather superficial ones you often get in organizations. You simply have to try harder at a distance.*

Again, just one model and there are many others.

References

Eco, U. *The Name of the Rose*.

Morris, S. and Willcocks, G. *Connecting with your Customers*, Pitman Publishing, London, 1996.

Slouka, M., see *The Guardian*, January 30, 1996.

Slouka, M. *War of the Worlds*.

chapter eight

ORGANIZATIONAL SKILLS FOR THE INFORMATION AGE – THE DILEMMAS

The challenge is to take the data overload and turn it into something positive

Introduction

Chapters five and six have focused on the personal skills that managers will need to develop to meet the demands of the information age. But what about organizations? How are they going to need to change in order to face the challenges?

The experts agree that change is essential:

> So far, most computer users still use the new technology to do faster what they have always done before. As soon, however, as the organization takes the first tentative steps from data to information, its decision processes, its management structure, and the way it gets work done, have to be transformed.

Peter Drucker,
*The New
Realities*

> An organization should use information to react more quickly than its competitors to a particular fact or circumstance. The organization which makes a strategic move first, if the move is correct, will improve and strengthen its position relative to its competitors.

Carol Cashmore
and Richard
Lyall,
*Business
Information
Systems and
Strategies*

But what is this likely to mean in practice? In this chapter and the next we explore some of the key ways in which organizations can gear themselves up for the information age.

We begin in this chapter from the perspective that organizations must make choices. There is no clear solution for all – instead there is a series of difficult decisions in response to a number of key dilemmas.

And the choices are quite stark. As the information revolution gathers pace, it will be the organizations that turn all the data they receive into knowledge that prosper. Secret corners and shaded information gardens in organizations are no longer simple inconveniences – they may threaten its very survival. The challenge is to take the data overload and turn it into something positive. This will take people and, of course, systems. One without the other will not work.

In the next chapter we go on to explore some key ways in which organizations can facilitate the change.

The dilemmas

The importance of information brings with it some dilemmas:

- Needing to balance sharing with security,
- Needing to balance centralization and devolution,
- Needing to balance volume with overload,
- Needing to balance specialism and generalism,
- Needing to balance downsizing with the premium on knowledge workers.

■ Sharing versus security

The first paradox centres around issues of security, secrecy, and confidentiality.

The problem occurs when necessary security seeps over into counterproductive secrecy.

Traditionally, organizations have tended to be secretive about information. Certain key information – for example, product designs, sensitive financial information, and so forth – has particular value to the organization and may have value to competitors. As organizations become increasingly aware of the value of information and knowledge there can be pressure to increase information security.

What is more, organizations have an obligation to respect confidentiality. Much information about staff, customers, and clients will often be sensitive. People don't want to feel that information about them is circulating out there. Laws restrict an organization's ability to share many kinds of personal information.

The problem occurs when necessary security seeps over into counterproductive secrecy. Organizations can develop a cultural mind set that seeks to restrict information sharing. For example, people may be pigeon-holed on a "need to know" basis, with information restricted to the in crowd and dripped begrudgingly to those beyond the magic circle.

It's worth referring back to Boisot's model of information cultures set out in chapter three. Boisot argues that certain organizational cultures – and in particular bureaucracies – develop strategies to restrict information sharing. They may physically control the flow of information, or they may use language that makes information highly inaccessible to those not in the know.

Also in chapter three, we introduced Davenport's models of information cultures. His notions of "monarchy" and "feudalism" are highly appropriate here, where either the top or the individual bits of the organization guard information privately to themselves. To quote Tom Peters, "information hoarding" has become commonplace within industry. Peters argues that it "will become a millstone round the neck" of tomorrow's organization.

Indeed, a culture of information secrecy runs counter to many of the demands that are now being placed on organizations – pressures to reduce hierarchy, devolve responsibility and decision making, and to empower people. Listen to some of the gurus of the new organization:

> "An individual without information cannot take responsibility; an individual who is given information cannot help but take responsibility."

Jan Carlzon, Director of Scandinavian Air Services

> There are few greater liberating forces than the sharing of information. There is no such thing as "delegation" or "motivation" without extensive information.

Tom Peters, *Thriving on Chaos*

> Communication is the third key to achieving synergies. Many opportunities for synergy come in the form of information sharing; thus, channels need to be established to enable managers and professionals from different business units and different parts of the organization to communicate.

Rosabeth Moss Kanter, *When Giants Learn to Dance*

Information sharing can support the new organization in many ways. The very concept of sharing information is a challenge to the old hierarchies and power structures. So any organization seeking to become more devolved and self-managing must from the outset eradicate information hoarding.

If staff throughout the organization are to take greater responsibility, they need information to take decisions, as Carlzon has pointed out. But giving people information has symbolic value as well – it is further proof that we really want them to take responsibility.

> **How can we ensure that people throughout the organization have the information they require, when they need it, while ensuring that information that should remain secure or confidential does not leak out?**

Information is also a bit like the money supply. As information circulates around the organization, it helps to generate more information. It prompts people to come up with new ideas, make linkages, and suggest improvements.

But if we are a looking at a future with organizations that resemble information democracies, what does that mean for the old ones where knowledge was power?

There's a very real dilemma here. How can we ensure that people throughout the organization have the information they require, when they need it, while ensuring that information that should remain secure or confidential does not leak out?

The dilemma becomes even more acute with the advent of partnerships, which depend upon frank and open information exchange. For example, Ford shares sales forecast information with its suppliers to enable them to plan production, but this information could be of value to competitors if it leaked wider.

So how do organizations cope with the security/sharing paradox? Here's one example:

Digital

Digital Equipment Corporation sees partnerships with suppliers as crucial. In the first place, purchasing represents a major cost element for the company which must be carefully controlled. Equally important has been the value of involving suppliers – of seeing them as an extension of the organization who both understand Digital's needs and can play an active role through suggesting ideas and improvements.

Digital recognises that effective partnership rests on information sharing, at several levels. At a strategic level, Digital will meet regularly with suppliers to discuss business plans and goals. At a planning level, Digital shares technical and forecasting knowledge and expertise. At an operational level Digital and its suppliers have integrated information systems to allow rapid and direct data exchange.

Where the company believes that certain information is too sensitive to share, it nonetheless expects boundary workers to explain why they are withholding information, and to be prepared to discuss and negotiate the issues involved so that partnership does not suffer.

Digital also believes that – while e-mail can be a vital medium for information exchange, it is not enough on its own. It even runs a helicopter service to bring people together, on the basis that people develop better relationships face-to-face.

Adapted from *When Giants Learn to Dance*, by Rosabeth Moss Kanter

It seems that organizations like Digital adopt a number of strategies to tackle the dilemma:

- They are very clear about which information is sensitive, and why. They have clear criteria for withholding information, whether from staff or from partner organizations, and make these criteria explicit. They are prepared to review and discuss the issue and modify their stance if this seems necessary.

- They manage relationships. There are rules about what can and cannot be discussed and disclosed to avoid potential problems with partners. For example, external consultants may be asked to sign a contract which explicitly sets standards for professional practice.

● Staff members learn that sharing information responsibly is a key aspect of their professional role. They know which information can be shared and which cannot. They are also well briefed about how to handle issues of sensitivity, whether with their own teams or in their relationships with partner organizations.

● Information systems are designed to support policy. Information that should be widely available is accessible on the system. Tools to restrict access such as passwords and user identities are used with restraint, and again people know why they are denied access to particular information.

Intranets again

In a recent seminar held by a top London design company participants from worldwide companies like Shell and Visa addressed the issue of how to share information.

The results were instructive. Participants pointed out that many organizations are establishing Intranets as the ideal way of sharing information. The Intranet really does have advantages. It gets information to people fast. It looks attractive. It has the buzz of the new. It is also a broadcast and a receptor medium. You can give information on it, but also field questions and get views. So it is interactive in all the right ways. And they can look absolutely fabulous.

They are rather like a living newsletter and they can have the liveliness inherent in this.

■ Centralization versus devolution

The second dilemma facing organizations in the information age is whether to centralize or devolve information management and systems.

Many early information systems were introduced in a highly ad hoc way. There might be a system for finance and another for payroll, completely unconnected. Individual departments would introduce systems that met their own needs with little concern for the wider organizational implications. As a result, different systems were likely to be incompatible. There was also a serious risk that data would be duplicated, and that customers would be continually asked for the same information time and again.

It's worth thinking back to Davenport's models of information cultures described in chapter three. Ad hoc systems tend to reflect a culture of what Davenport calls "anarchy," where a lack of overall policy and co-ordination leads to individuals having to obtain and manage their own information. Or as Tapscott and Caston argue:

> The isolated technology applications of an earlier time are no longer adequate. Companies are discovering that they have to create enterprise capabilities that will create new opportunities for sharing and reusing information and information technology resources at all levels. There is a growing need for direct links between the sources of information and the people who use it and for ways of sharing this information throughout the organization.

D. Tapscott and A. Caston
Paradigm Shift: The New Promise of Information Technology

As computing power has increased, so the scope to integrate systems has grown, and organizations can now seek a total computing solution – a centralized, integrated information system serving the whole organization. But while this brings immense opportunities, it also carries potential threats.

A centralized system is likely to be characterized by a number of features:

- Organizationwide strategy, policy and approach to managing information and information technology, with a tendency to top-down implementation.

- Centralized decision making about systems, software, and access.

- A strong central IT department distinct from the rest of the organization.

- Computing power will be centralized with huge databases and mainframes, and users across the organization working on basic or even "dumb" terminals.

Centralized systems often spring from what in chapter three we termed a technical approach to information design, and accompany what Davenport calls "technocratic utopianism," where there is a strong belief that it is possible to model the information flows of the organization, and that technology represents a key solution to problems.

Centralized, integrated systems have many attractions. They can ensure a coherent approach to IT across the organization. They offer immense scope for information exchange, with potential for people to bring together information from a range of sources. They reduce the risk of anarchy, eliminating the incompatible ad hoc systems which might otherwise be scattered throughout the organization.

Rank Xerox

Rank Xerox engineers spend most of their time out on the road visiting customers and maintaining their photocopiers and other equipment. They take with them small, hand-held computers which they can plug directly into a customer's 'phone socket.

Using the computer they can update the customer's record, order parts, and check details of prices and availability. The computer is simple to use and it is straightforward for the engineer to order a part or check a price.

The computer also helps communication with the engineer's central office – messages can be sent to and from the engineer so that they know about any changes in their schedule for the day.

Spar Stores

Grocers who run Spar stores across the UK have the opportunity to use electronic data interchange – EDI – to help them manage their stores. EDI simply means that different computers can communicate electronically – the store computer is connected via a modem with the supplier's computer – data can be sent from the store directly to the supplier, or vice versa.

Checkout scanners read the bar codes on products to produce a bill for the customer. The store computer also uses this information to monitor stock. If necessary extra stock is reordered automatically from the supplier via the modem.

In addition, the system provides the storekeeper with extra information including price changes and financial information such as profitability of different goods and shelves.

On the other hand, when poorly designed or implemented they have brought enormous problems. Some examples, quoted in *Computer Weekly*, include:

- The UK stock exchange introduced an information system (named TAURUS) which would mean that sales of equities could be settled in real time. Previously it could take several weeks to settle. However the system turned into a "£75m fiasco"

  (*Computer Weekly*, 28 April 94).

- The furniture suppliers Saxon Hawk spent £245,000 on a computer system designed to feed better information about stock and sales performance from its 40 stores to headquarters. Group Finance Director Robert Adams dubbed the system "a disaster."

  (*Computer Weekly*, 21 May 92).

- When the UK introduced a new local tax known as the "poll tax," there were major backlogs in processing payment. Local councils blamed these partly on problems in introducing new computerized databases.

  (*Computer Weekly*, 3 Sept. 92).

- California's Department of Motor Vehicles scrapped a contract to link separate databases together, writing off £30m of taxpayers' money.

  (*Computer Weekly*, 12 May 94).

Problems with highly centralized systems can also arise from the way they may ape traditional hierarchies. A centralized system may emphasise control rather than responsibility, conformity rather than initiative.

As Tony Knight and David Silk put it:

Tony Knight
and David Silk,
*Managing
Information*

> An effective information system cannot be constrained by formal channels of information flow – up the line of functional command to a senior manager and down to another functional line. Rather it will facilitate the establishment of a flexible organization which is able to respond quickly to any change in the internal or external business environments.

Dissatisfaction with centralized systems has led some organizations to turn to more "devolved" systems which reduce the stress on control and increase the emphasis on coordination.

A devolved system will have a number of key characteristics:

- There will remain a clear overall strategy. However this will be developed on a more negotiated, consensual basis, and will represent a framework rather than a detailed blueprint.

- More detailed decision making will be devolved to individual bits of the organization. There is an emphasis on "interfacing" rather than integrating – there is greater scope for teams to manage their own information needs in ways that blend with those elsewhere in the organization.

● There will remain a team of IT specialists. However, they are more likely to see themselves as internal suppliers, whose role is to service the needs of their internal customers – in other words, IT users throughout the organization.

● A higher proportion of computing power will be devolved through the organization. In the early stages this may involve users working on personal computers with direct access to key software. As devolution increases it is likely to involve work group computing, with small networks servicing teams.

> Problems with highly centralized systems can also arise from the way they may ape traditional hierarchies. A centralized system may emphasise control rather than responsibility, conformity rather than initiative.

This model often accompanies what Davenport calls a culture of "federalism," where information management is based on consensus and negotiation about information flows.

This box summarizes the key distinctions between centralized and devolved systems.

Aspect	Centralized	Devolved
Strategy	Decided at the top	Decided in consultation and partnership
Systems	Unified, integrated	Federal, interfacing
Specialists	Powerful, distinct part of organization, decide for others	Internal suppliers, act as supporters and facilitators
Computing power	Most power found in the center in the form of minis and mainframes	Users have direct access to more power via PCs and work group computing

So once again, there's a dilemma here. How can an organization grasp the benefits that accompany centralized information systems – the sense of coherence and strategy, the value of integration, and communication – without these sapping the creative energy of devolved, self-managing teams?

Or, to put it the other way round, how can the organization allow users sufficient ownership, flexibility and scope to develop without risking a return to anarchy?

Some of the lessons from successful organizations here seem to be:

- They seek to align information strategy with organizational culture and other strategic initiatives. The organization has a clear sense of direction – it knows what it wants to change, and how. So where there is a need to devolve responsibility, this will be supported both by devolved IT and increased information sharing.

- They create an infrastructure which supports users without dominating them. Users have the IT facilities and power to manage their own information and to develop systems in ways that suit them without running counter to wider organizational needs.

- Everything supports empowerment. Systems are easy to learn and use. Comprehensive training and support is provided with the aim of helping users to become full members of the information age. IT staff have a customer-oriented, needs-focussed mind set.

■ Volume versus overload

We have already stressed how managers must develop the personal skills to access and filter information – how they need to be able to make sense of the everincreasing information flood.

A similar dilemma faces the whole organization. How can the organization remain open and welcoming to new information, without becoming swamped by it?

On the one hand, there is a clear imperative on organizations to bring in information. This is driven by several factors:

- The need to interact fully with the environment. Organizations need information if they are both to monitor and adapt to external changes, whether economic, political, social, or technological, and to actively seek to modify the environment.

- The need to be closer to customers. If organizations are to respond more quickly and effectively to changes in customers requirements, they need up-to-date, accurate information about their customers.

- The increasing importance of partnership. The need to work more closely with other organizations also creates a need for more information. We need information about other organizations in order to identify potential partners. And as we saw earlier, once we work in partnership we will need to bring in massive amounts of information from our partners.

- The need to remain competitive. As information becomes more and more important to organizations, so the risk increases that competitors will get the information first. As Carol Cashmore commented in the quote at the start of this chapter, an organization "should use information to react more quickly than its competitors."

The business imperative for more information runs parallel to the fact that there is so much more information out there. And organizations are responding by bringing in as much information as possible.

However, this weight of information can place enormous stress on an organization and its systems. The problem is this. You can import more information into the organization, but this risks slowing down the organization's decision-making powers. Like the weeds in the Sargasso Sea, information can clog the corporate propellers and bring us to an undignified standstill.

Information overload can lead to several problems. In extreme cases it may result in system failure or collapse. Databases crammed with information become slow to access. There is already evidence that parts of the Internet are creaking under the strain, with unacceptable access times during peak periods. One hospital saw its most important information disappear into cyber-space as a major system crash erased thousands of vital patient records.

More commonly, overload leads to information being unused or underused. Valuable information about customers may be collected but lie unused because insufficient thought has been given to managing it, or because staff do not know what to do with it. Examples come from many sectors. In banking, for example, Mike Hartley (1995) has argued:

Mike Hartley,
Coopers &
Lybrand Digest

> The knowledge asset of organizations is not being expanded or tapped to anything like its full potential. Raw data needs to be validated and structured before it becomes useful information, and this can involve significant effort. Many banks have found that new sources of information are in practice underused, with people not fully aware of what is available and how it could improve their work and enrich decision making.

So, how do organizations come to terms with the problems and limit the risks involved? Short of putting up the barricades, how can we stem the information flood and divert it into value? Once more, successful organizations seem to be taking a number of steps:

- They develop filtering mechanisms. They look for ways of screening out unwanted data and making sense of potentially confusing or contradictory information. They develop a customer focus which ensures that everyone knows what everyone else needs.

- They develop systems that can ensure the right information goes to the right person or is stored in an appropriate form and manner. The data warehousing model described in chapter three gives one example of how organizations can accommodate the exponential growth in information by creating channels for bringing in information and storing or passing it on to customers.

- They develop the personal skills, both of those boundary workers at the interface who have a proactive role to play in importing information, and the people who handle information, sift, synthesize and prepare it for use, and work as liaison points between the departments.

- They use up-to-date technology solutions to support the collection, processing and channeling of information. In particular, they seek appropriate ways of coding and identifying information so that it can be accessed readily by the people who need it, using a delivery channel that is appropriate.

■ Specialism versus generalism

Increasingly, organizations are recognizing the value of knowledge. But what kind of knowledge do we need, and what species of knowledge worker do we seek to employ? Is it the specialist knowledge that comes from knowing a topic in depth? Or is it the generalist knowledge that comes from broader experience?

Specialism brings many benefits. Specialists have the time to develop a detailed perspective, and to hone specific skills. They contribute the in-depth grasp of a topic that in many areas is essential.

> If your ear aches, are you better off consulting the ear, nose and throat surgeon who knows everything there is to be known about ears? Or should you go to a holistic practitioner who can spot the links with your teeth, your lifestyle, and your diet?

But specialism can bring rigidity, a narrow focus, a lack of perspective. Ask a specialist about something outside his or her area and the chances are that he or she won't know the answer. Generalists may not know the detail – but they may be able to spot links between apparently unconnected events, draw together conflicting approaches and philosophies, and above all take an overview, a broader perspective.

The dilemma is common to many areas. If your ear aches, are you better off consulting the ear, nose and throat surgeon who knows everything there is to be known about ears? Or should you go to a holistic practitioner who can spot the links with your teeth, your lifestyle, and your diet?

The dilemma faces publishers as well. Who is the best writer – the subject specialist who may have limited writing skills, or the professional writer who has a broader perspective, but will need time to develop more than a superficial view of the topic?

Organizations have for too long ducked this issue. They appoint technical specialists to managerial positions without equipping them to become managers. Or they bring in managers who have succeeded elsewhere, but who know nothing about what the company does. In either case, it's sink or swim – you learn very fast or you go down with the ship. The symptoms are commonplace – people promoted out of incompetence; gripes about middle managers who can't manage; costly errors that arise from lack of technical expertise. And when one approach fails, it's common to veer to the other extreme.

The problems are often exacerbated by reward policy and structure. In an organization where the only way to earn more is to move up the hierarchy, it is normal for those with specialist technical knowledge to see management as the profitable career move.

Town planning departments of local government in the UK are a typical example of this problem. Planners generally have a specialist qualification. They belong to the appropriate professional institute. They progress through the profession as they develop more advanced, technical knowledge. Their professional skills and expertise are invaluable to the local authority.

The problem comes when planners reach the point in the career ladder where the only promotion is to become managers. They receive little or no management training and preparation. They have become used to working alone and may be loathe to take on the role of leading a team.

As a result, the local authority loses valuable specialist expertise without gaining the benefit of generalist skills. The planner-manager may lose much of what made the job attractive. The team lacks cohesion and vision. The only solution may be early retirement, the ultimate waste of potential.

In *The Age of Unreason* Charles Handy predicts that it will become harder and harder for people to maintain themselves solely or principally as specialists. He argues:

> Everyone in the core will have to be a manager while at the same time no-one can afford to be only a manager. Smaller numbers in the core require more flexibility and more responsibility. Everyone will increasingly be expected not only to have their own professional or technical expertise, but will also very rapidly acquire responsibility for money, people or projects, a managerial task, in other words.

Charles Handy,
The Age of Unreason

Organizations grappling with the problem have reached for a range of solutions:

- They develop a clear policy for development and succession. They know what balance of specialist and generalist expertise they want in their workforce in one, five, ten years' time, and they have plans for getting there. They are clear about where gaps exist, and how they will fill them. They are not afraid to confront the power of professionals. Above all, they know how they want to develop their managers and their teams.

- They design teams that blend specialist and generalist expertise. Within teams people have clear roles to play which reflect their background. But they can also learn and share skills, with individuals developing into more rounded professionals.

● They design and operate a reward structure that values contribution. An organization that values both specialism and generalism will reward both in appropriate ways. People can be paid more for getting better at their specialism, without having to jump into management. They may get bonuses for acquiring new skills or new gradings for developing their own specialist competence. Stuctures for rewarding teams can ensure that everyone, generalist or specialist, can share in the results of success.

And of course some of the barriers, the language that has valued specialism, as opposed to generalism, are being washed away.

■ In-house versus subcontracting

The specialist–generalist dilemma is in fact just one dimension of the wider choice facing organizations – just how big should we be, and who do we see as our key workers?

The recent trend in organizations has been toward "downsizing," "restructuring" or "skinnying down." The search is on for the leaner, more flexible, and more competitive corporation. More and more organizations are concentrating core expertise in-house, drawing in low-risk expertise from outside through partnerships and consultancies.

Charles Handy has described some of the new ways of working such as the "shamrock" organization – with three strands of core team, the subcontractors and the flexible labor force of part-time and flexible people – or the "doughnut" organization, made up of a federation of interdependent but self-managing units. In federal organizations "the drive and energy come from the bits, with the centre an influencing force, relatively low in profile" (Handy, 1989).

But what happens to the prized knowledge workers in all this? To what extent do information champions belong to the corporate in-house team? To what extent do they become part of the subcontracting pool, free to sell their knowledge to the highest bidder, or the "bits" that provide the drive and energy?

The arguments for retaining knowledge and expertise in-house are many. It is easier to generate loyalty and commitment among permanent staff. They

> Cost is a key element – while consultants may charge more per day than permanent staff, they can be brought in as needed, reducing the permanent salary bill.

are available constantly, and are not torn away through commitments to other organizations. The organization can develop their skills, knowledge, and expertise in a planned and coherent manner. In-house staff are there at those invaluable ad hoc moments when unexpected ideas are generated and synergies forged.

However, there is also a strong case for buying in knowledge. Cost is a key element – while consultants may charge more per day than permanent staff, they can be brought in as needed, reducing the permanent salary bill. An organization may be able to develop a far larger pool for people than it could ever afford in-house. But there are other benefits as well. Consultants working with other organizations develop a width of experience and knowledge that is hard for corporate staff to obtain. They bring a fresh perspective to the organization, less hindered by custom and tradition.

The very nature of knowledge workers creates twin, opposing forces here. On the one hand, knowledge workers are the ultimate professionals. They are superbly equipped for the self-managing world of consultancy. They have honed the art of managing the customer and meeting their requirements. They are quick learners and can be expected to contribute to a new team from day one. All this makes it easy to draw knowledge workers from the wider team.

But on the other hand, they are people who seek influence. They want to make a mark. They can see where things are going wrong and they want to create improvements. And as they are good team players they can play a crucial role at the very summit of the organization. All this strengthens the case for maintaining knowledge workers at the core of the organization.

So how does the successful organization strike yet another difficult balance?

- They have a proper strategy for people management. They identify and review the competences that the organization needs and clarify which of these should be internal and which should be bought in. They have long-term plans to develop these competences, both in their own staff and in consultants, subcontractors and suppliers.

- They actively seek to blur the edges around the organization. They offer their consultants, subcontractors, and suppliers many of the benefits of full membership, whether by involving them in planning, providing development opportunities, or by inviting them to Christmas lunch.

- They actively seek to inspire loyalty and commitment from both the core team and the privileged outsiders.

The concept of organizational skills

So what's the upshot of all this? What this chapter has shown is that, in confronting the dilemmas facing them, organizations are developing a range of responses. And from these various responses, it is possible to identify some key underlying threads – in effect a number of skills that organizations need to acquire and refine if they are to succeed in the information age.

The first conclusion we can draw is that the challenges facing organizations are complex, and may indeed be more complex than we can readily conceive. As Gareth Morgan has commented:

I believe that some of the most fundamental problems we face stem from the fact that the complexity and sophistication of our thinking do not match the complexity and sophistication of the realities with which we have to deal.

Gareth Morgan,
*Images of
Organisation*

There is no ready-made solution that can be picked up from organization A and transferred wholesale into organization B. Indeed any solution that does not take full account of the context, customers, staff, and culture of the organization is doomed to failure. To quote Morgan again, "the result is that our actions are often simplistic, and at times downright harmful."

This means that the first skill organizations need is the creative power to form a **clear vision and strategy**. They must be able to do this at the overall level, of where they want the organization to go and how they want it to develop. They must also be able to align this overall vision with clear strategies for planning and managing both people and information. The organizational skills of visioning are therefore at the top of the agenda.

> This means that the first skill organizations need is the creative power to form a clear vision and strategy.

Leading on from this are two clear consequences. First, organizations need the skills to design, develop and use **systems and technology** in ways that support the overall strategy. And they need to do this in a manner that is at the same time flexible and organizationwide. No longer can we call in the IT experts to solve our technical problems – we must all bring to bear our vital generalist skills alongside those of the IT specialists to create solutions that work throughout the organization.

Secondly, organizations need the skills to grow and develop **people,** again clearly in line with overall strategy and direction. This does not just mean training as it used to be known – indeed training may become a much less important part of the operation. It means creating a culture and environment for learning and putting in place the supports that ensure people can learn continually. It needs to be clear that the organization actually values learning and intends to use the collective knowledge it gains.

Finally, organizations will increasingly need much more sophisticated information handling skills. They need to get better at **sharing, filtering,** and **adding meaning.**

A final horror

This is a true story. A large international company advertized for a junior IT person. The job had a salary of about $20,000 a year. The director in charge of the recruitment established a horrific recruitment interview including tests, role plays, simulations, and the like. He had at his side three $1,700 a day top-notch computer consultants to take the people through their paces. He had the consultants in case the appointee strayed into areas of jargon and experience that he himself was unfamiliar with. In simple terms, the information revolution has spawned new areas of pseudo knowledge that can scare the pants off organizations.

If though expertise and knowledge had been shared within the team the need for the consultants would have evaporated along with a large bill.

Chapter nine will go on to explore these skills in greater depth.

References

Boisot, M. *Information and Organisations: The Manager as Anthropologist,* Fontana, London, 1987.

Cashmore, C. and Lyall, R. *Business Information Systems and Strategies,* Prentice Hall, 1991.

Davenport, T., Eccles, R. and Prusak, L. "Information politics" in *Sloan Management Review,* Fall 1992.

Drucker, P. *The New Realities,* Mandarin. London, 1989.

Handy, C. *The Age of Unreason,* Business Books, 1989.

Hartley, M. *Coopers and Lybrand Bankers Digest,* Summer 1995.

Knight, T. and Silk, D. *Managing Information,* McGraw Hill, 1990.

Morgan, G. *Images of Organization*, Sage, 1986.

Moss Kanter, R. *When Giants Learn to Dance*, Unwin, 1989.

Peters, T. *Thriving on Chaos*, Pan, 1987.

Tapscott, D. and Caston, A. *Paradigm Shift: The New Promise of Information Technology*, McGraw Hill, 1993.

ORGANIZATIONAL SKILLS FOR THE INFORMATION AGE – THE REALITIES

Just what kind of organization
is fit for the information age?

Introduction

Chapter eight concluded that the complexity of the dilemmas facing organizations is very real. In Gareth Morgan's words (1986), organizations need the skills to "confront and manage contradiction and paradox, not pretend they do not exist."

This chapter focuses on these key organizational skills, namely:

- The need for vision,
- The need to design, develop, and use systems and technology,
- The need to grow and develop people,
- The need for advanced information handling skills – sharing, filtering, and adding meaning.

What is abundantly clear is the company that stays still and does not think through how it will manage the information will wither and die. And this means that some very big companies will surely go by the board in the coming years as they fail to adapt to the challenges that face them.

> We need to be able to use a range of myths and metaphors to describe and explain what we see, and envision new ways of working and acting.

The need for vision

The most important message to emerge so far is the need for strategic vision. Without vision, an organization cannot expect to make the most of the information age.

It certainly can't expect to survive in the infochaos that has resulted.

■ Using myths and metaphors

Vision is crucial on a number of levels. It is fundamental to creating a view of the organization. We need to be able to use a range of myths and metaphors to describe and explain what we see, and envision new ways of working and acting.

Gareth Morgan has coined the term "imaginization" to illuminate this process of envisioning the changing organization and of conveying just how powerful images and ideas can be in shaping organizations. In his book, *Images of Organisation*, he argues:

Gareth Morgan,
Images of
Organisation

> When we think about organisation in this manner we are provided with a constant reminder that we are in a creative process where new images and ideas can create new actions. ... We recognise that the way we "read" organisations influences how we produce them.

Morgan describes a number of metaphors for interpreting and changing organizations, some of which we have met earlier in this book:

Morgan's metaphors for organizations

- Organizations as machines,
- Organizations as organisms,
- Organizations as brains,
- Organizations as cultures,
- Organizations as political systems,
- Organizations as psychic prisons,
- Organization as flux and transformation,
- Organizations as instruments of domination.

Adapted from *Images of Organisation*, by Gareth Morgan

Few of us are used to consciously envisioning or imaginizing organizations. But this skill is going to become more and more crucial to organizational survival.

Let's follow the argument through. We are now clear that information and knowledge are central to organizations on two levels. On one level, the importance and volume of information is forcing organizations to develop systems that import, manage and export it effectively. On another level, information and knowledge are providing an increasing proportion of the added value of the products and services that organizations offer.

Yet, as we saw in chapter one, information is not a tangible asset or resource. It is not something we can send down the production line or package in a box. The value of information only becomes apparent when we interact with it, when we use it for thinking. The knowledge organization is built, not of concrete things, but of ideas and imagination.

All this means that the capacity to imagine, to visualize, to picture and indeed to dream are no longer the sole domain of artists and writers. Tomorrow's chief executive will only be employable if he or she can reflect on and transform information to envision the future.

We have gone in for a spot of envisioning ourselves.

■ Building a new kind of organization

Just what kind of organization is fit for the information age? Surely not the traditional bureaucracy with its rank and status and its locked filing cabinets. Nor also the organization that fritters away the information and knowledge it has – happy to let staff leave because someone else will always come along.

No, we need to envision what the knowledge organization will look and feel like. It's only when we construct a model that we can begin to build on it, examine it and make concrete some of the airy notions that bedevil the information age. So let's try.

For a start, the organization will work on its culture.

In this new organization, knowledge will be valued and the contribution each can make to that knowledge will be encouraged and rewarded. In this organization, sharing of information will be a passport to greater things. Information champions get on, the anally retentive hoarders and hiders will be nowhere. Knowledge may be power, but sharing knowledge is greater power still in this new organization.

But how at an organizational level do we do this? Well, it's likely that knowledge and the sharing of it will explicitly be in people's targets (more of which later). And information will be shared freely. And as for those who won't play ball, well, they may have their rights to keeping information taken away. If you can't share your organization's most valuable resource, then you shouldn't be allowed to be a gatekeeper of it. So maybe in this organization we are inventing a situation where those who won't share lose access to the gatekeeper role, and it is given to someone else, or taken back to the center.

> **Knowledge may be power, but sharing knowledge is greater power still in this new organization.**

All in all, the organization will value learning and do all it can to facilitate it.

In this new organization there may be new roles established. We might get information hunters and brokers who seek out information and help bring it back to the organization. But we won't get information gathering seen as someone else's job. Everyone will be an information champion. There will certainly be expertise on-call to help whenever it is needed.

But what is for sure is that the new organization will have listening posts everywhere. Not in a sinister way, you understand, but just able to find out, be in touch, stay abreast. The organization that encourages everyone to stay in touch with each other but not the world will wither and die. In our new organization all employees could well get access to an hour's time on the Net daily – why not be in touch with the world? And this approach will be sanctioned by the organization – not a furtive activity.

> **In our new organization all employees could well get access to an hour's time on the Net daily .**

A large European hotel chain recently decided that its employees were spending too much time indoors. As well as being bad for the complexion, it was bad for business. People indoors are not in touch with information. So it set up a program whereby every single member of staff had to spend some time each week visiting competitor hotels and talking to customers. They also encouraged people to read the press, keep abreast, and generally get tuned in to the information around them. In our new organization, time spent outside listening will be welcomed. The organization will have a big travel budget because staff will be encouraged to get out there, find out what's what, learn, and bring it back to base. And people will be given time – time to get plugged into the world.

And what else?

There will be an infrastructure designed to help make sense of the information chaos. There may be a data warehouse, but only if appropriate. There are likely to be databases to help synthesize information. There is certain to be work on technical interfaces to make accessing and using information easy, straightforward and user-friendly. The organization may develop its own browsers and computer interfaces so the people don't get the information raw.

And then there's the acting on the information. Information is not knowledge until it is used. So the new organization will actively seek to do something with the knowledge it gains. It will demonstrate that it is worth sharing information because the organization uses it and values it. And the information will be delivered fast to the point at which it is needed – those who take the decisions.

And day to day? Well, new technology will be used where appropriate. People will be trained so they are comfortable with the basic packages but encouraged to learn and keep learning. In the new organization the only person not to understand a computer will not be the CEO. Everyone will be part of the new age not just the minions. But the new will not be shunned or sought for its own sake.

> ### Euro 96
>
> In the recent soccer tournament in England a new innovation was introduced. In the old days when a player was substituted, the team's trainer held up a simple board with the number of the player who was to come off. Not so in whizzy, modern Euro 96. No, the dear old board which had served the game for 100 years was replaced with a hand-held electronic board. Not such a good idea when the sun's reflection makes it impossible to see the number. They should have stuck with the board.

And the result is that the organization does not deny the chaos and overload around it, but accepts it, enjoys it, and develops the skills to thrive in it. It goes into the age as an organization.

Sound too good to be true? Well, maybe, but let's look at some of the organizational skills in more detail anyway.

A final thought on this. One of the trends that all the people we interviewed for this book told us about was the trend toward customization. The wealth of information available, properly sorted and used, should allow even big companies to offer a truly customized service. So the new organization will learn and grow and use the information always to improve what it offers based on up-to-the second (literally) knowledge of what customers want.

■ Bringing a creative perspective to business strategy

This has several implications for the development of strategy. In the first place, as organizations develop their business strategy they need the capacity to "create the future" (Eskin 1992). We need to go beyond describing what is already there. We need to create a dynamic vision of where the organization will be in the future, and the role that knowledge and information will play in this.

Secondly, there is growing consensus that strategy must be developed as a participative activity, one that involves all the knowledge workers and may involve the wider team as well. As Handy (1989) comments, intelligent people prefer to agree than obey. Organizations must be prepared to cope with the discussion, tension, and conflict that this involves, because this is the way to gaining eventual consensus and ownership and a shared view of the future.

And thirdly, strategy must be an evolving activity. Pedler, Burgoyne, and Boydell, leading UK writers on learning organizations, call for policy and strategy formulation to be structured as a learning process, with business plans formulated and revised as you go along:

> Managerial acts are thus seen as conscious experiments, rather than set solutions. Deliberate small-scale experiments and feedback loops are built into the planning process to enable continuous improvement in the light of experience.

M. Pedler,
J. Burgoine, and
T. Boydell,
The Learning Company

In order to envision strategy, organizations fundamentally need to be able to ask deep and probing questions. Here are some examples.

Key questions for envisioning strategy

Looking at ourselves

- *How do we see ourselves? What myths and metaphors do we use to describe the organization?*
- *What kind of organization do we want to be? Which words and images can we use to describe it?*
- *How do we see our people? Does it help to use words like responsible, resourceful, creative … ?*
- *What are we good at? What do we like about ourselves? How do we want others to see us?*

Challenging impossibility

- *What is now commonplace that seemed impossible five/ten years ago?*

- *What is the most unlikely scenario for the next ten years? What will stop it happening?*
- *If we were to change one thing in order to really delight our customers, what would it be? What must we do to change it?*
- *What's the biggest problem we all face? What must we do to change it?*

Pushing back the frontiers

- *What if … we could do everything differently?*
- *What if…we always asked customers what they think?*

And it is the ability to keep asking and answering questions like this that will help the organization learn and continue to learn?

■ Aligning the information strategy

It follows that any strategy for managing information must fall out of the wider organizational vision and strategy. In Victor Peel's words, an information strategy "should be aimed at ensuring that its information systems and information technology are linked to and support its objectives."

> Technology is the concrete, visible side of information. Tied as we are to our dependence on things, it is tempting to leap on to the technology bandwagon.

Far too often this is not the case. Chris Edwards (1991) has shown how organizations all too often entrust the development of information strategy to IT specialists, or even to outside IT consultants. As a direct result, information strategies, where they exist, may be little more than wish lists or plans for introducing someone's pet technology. As such, they are often poorly informed by business priorities, unlikely to be owned throughout the organization, and often difficult to implement.

It's easy to understand why this is the case. Technology is the concrete, visible side of information. Tied as we are to our dependence on things, it is tempting to leap on to the technology bandwagon. It avoids facing up to the intangible reality of information.

However, this is to ignore again the fact that information only has value in interaction with people. As Adams *et al.* argue, information strategy must align not just with the overall business strategy, but also with a clear human resources strategy:

> Information only has value in interaction with people.

Paul Adams,
Mike Conway,
and
Nick Owens,
The Strategic Use of Information Systems and Technology

> Achieving an effective organisation cannot be accomplished by the information strategy and the application of IT alone – it requires an approach which involves the combination of business strategy together with information and human resources.

> Even if the organisation has a well prepared business strategy, supported by a well planned information systems and technology strategy, this can fail if the organisation's culture, values, beliefs and attitudes do not match these other two strategies.

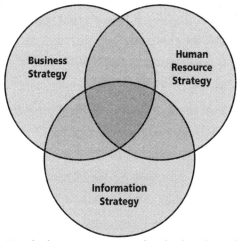

from: *The Strategic Use of Information Systems and Technology,* by Paul Adams, Mike Conway and Nick Owens, 1992

Some more questions

- *Go on – can you imagine the perfect information system?*
- *In what ways is the formal information system better than the grapevine? Honestly?*
- *Which bits of our information system get in our way? How can we change them?*
- *Imagine an invisible information system. What would it be like?*

Design, develop, and use systems and technology

Chapter eight argued that the highly centralized information systems that developed as computing power and scope for integration increased may not always be appropriate to the information organization staffed by knowledge workers. But this is not to deny the value of information technology – quite the contrary. As computing and telecommunications have gone on evolving, so new systems have emerged that may be more appropriate to our needs.

In *Paradigm Shift: The New Promise of Information Technology*, Don Tapscott and Art Caston draw parallels between how organizations are changing, and how developments in systems and technology may support these changes. They actually put the technology themes first – we believe that the organization must come first. However their analysis provides an invaluable summary of all that is changing in the world of information technology and systems (see table opposite).

All this means that the tools information champions need are now available, and will go on improving rapidly. Organizations, therefore, need the skills to select appropriate technologies and design systems that support the creative management of information.

- **Start from the vision.** Always start with the vision and the strategy, never with the technology. Set out clearly what you want the technology to achieve, without constraining yourself by past experience.

- **Put people first.** It's the information champions who will make the new organization succeed. They must be involved in determining what the system is able to do.

- **Dinosaurs couldn't evolve.** Technology is costly. There's much to be said for working with existing systems. But just as the point came when T-Rex was not up to the job, so the first and second generation computing technology may no longer do what you need.

How the new technologies can support the new organization

Organizational theme	Technology theme
Openness. Organizations are becoming more open, both in how they are structured internally and in their relationships with other organizations	*Open systems* offer greater scope to move from one hardware platform to another
Integration. Organizations are becoming more integrated and seamless, with fewer barriers between departments and activities	*Networking* facilitates communication and sharing of information
Empowerment. Individuals and teams are increasingly empowered to act and create value	*Distributed computing* transfers the computer power from the center to the user
Immediacy. Organizations must be able to continually and immediately adjust to changing business conditions	*Real time* technology means that databanks can be updated the instant a transaction has gone through
Cooperation. The emphasis of the new organization is on cooperation and interdependence	*Cooperative processing* through client and server devices
Commitment. Organizations must now rely more on commitment and less on control	*Rules and protocols* will increasingly be determined by users themselves
Organizational independence. The self-managing team is becoming the key unit of business development.	*Architectural modularity* means that independent parts of a system can be grouped together
Competence building. Organizations must find professional pathways for knowledge workers	*Platform specialization* allows the new hardware to be customized to meet the needs of individuals and teams
Accessibility. Increasingly, knowledge workers need access to information and decision making	*User-friendly* systems create greater access as they are easy both to learn and to use
Time and space independence. As the corporation becomes international, it must be able to cope with working across distance and time zones	*Global networking* supports communication across both space and time

Adapted from *Paradigm Shift: The New Promise of Information Technology*, by Don Tapscott and Art Caston

A participative approach to designing information systems

1 Clarify why you need to change.
2 Define system boundaries.
3 Describe existing system.
4 Define key objectives of new system.
5 Define key tasks.
6 Specify key information needs.
7 Diagnose weaknesses.
8 Diagnose job needs.
9 Specify organizational design.
10 Identify technical options.
11 Specify work design.
12 Implement.
13 Evaluate.

Adapted from *Designing Participatively*, by E. Mumford.

So there will be systems because systems are the infrastructure around which learning can take place. But beware – if we accept that the information age is characterized by excess, overload, and information gluttony – then new models will constantly be needed, and in the final analysis none may prove to be sufficient.

A top-rate system

A transnational direct financial company has used the most modern system to make sure it is never short of information. Call the company from anywhere in Europe and you get though to someone from the company within three rings. This person may be sitting in the company HQ or sitting in their own living room because the company has invested in an amazing telecommunications system that means that if you ring and all the HQ lines are busy your call is automatically switched to one of an army of homeworkers ready to take your call.

Grow and develop people

Given what we've said so far in this chapter, it follows that a crucial task for the organization is to develop its people effectively. It's all very well saying that everyone must be involved in strategy development, technology selection, and systems planning, but such activities demand high levels of competence. People must be developed and supported if they are to make a full contribution.

In any case, the concept of the learning organization introduced in chapter four highlights the need for a structure and culture that support continuous learning throughout the organization. As Charles Handy puts it:

> The organisation's thinking or "intellective" capacity has [to be] increased. In this vision, the organization is full of colleagues and co-learners, its thinking skill becomes its most precious resource, and the challenge of keeping that skill upgraded the major task of the organization. It really has to be a sort of corporate university.

Charles Handy,
The Age of
Unreason

The task is considerable. To recap on some key issues:

- Staff members need comprehensive training and support if they are to become full members of the information age. They need to be able to share information responsibly and to handle issues of sensitivity. They need to develop the personal skills of importing, handling, sifting, synthesizing, and preparing information for use. Many of the skills described in chapters five and six will be crucial.

- The organization needs a clear policy for development and succession, clarifying the required balance of specialist and generalist expertise, and identifying and reviewing the competences that the organization needs.

To deliver all this calls for action on a number of levels. There must be a clear commitment to learning throughout the organization, with the organization recognizing just how crucial it is for future success. To quote Handy again:

> To expect the intelligent executive to devote one fifth (one day a week) of his or her time preparing themselves for a different and a better future would not be unreasonable in the new organization.

Charles Handy,
*The Age of
Unreason*

In other words, the organization must value learning and give it priority. It is no longer good enough to say that production or delivery can take priority over learning – if learning is not a top priority then the organization will not learn and if the organization does not learn, it will be unable to survive.

In order to do this, we must fundamentally reconsider how we go about learning. Traditional off-the-job courses will still have a role to play in equipping people with certain basic skills and knowledge. However, we must not expect them to play a major role in developing the new organization. The most important learning that people need today cannot be found in a training room – it is out there in the workplace, in the day-to-day contact with colleagues and customers, in reflection on how well things have worked.

The challenge is, therefore, how to harness this real-life learning. And the secret lies in making people effective, self-managing learners. Central is the idea of the "reflective practitioner" coined by Schön (1983). Schön observed how professionals reacted to something that fell outside the range of ordinary expectations. He describes an investment banker who sensed that something was wrong by the way a client talked to him, even though the client's figures seemed fine – but the client went bankrupt soon afterwards. Or the ophthalmologist, confronted with a patient suffering from two eye disorders, who found that removing all treatment actually cured one of the disorders.

The challenge is, therefore, how to harness this real-life learning. And the secret lies in making people effective, self-managing learners.

In each case, the practitioner allows himself to experience surprise, puzzlement or confusion in a situation which he finds uncertain or unique. He reflects on the phenomena before him, and on the prior understandings which have been implicit in his behaviour. He carries out an experiment which serves to generate both a new understanding of the phenomena and a change in the situation.

Donald Schön,
*The Reflective
Practitioner*

These capabilities seem exactly what information organizations need to develop in their people. We need to help people to become "researchers in practice," people who can:

- **Feel comfortable when they encounter uncertainty** – if people are to behave effectively in the face of new and very different challenges, they need to recognize that each new situation may be unique. It is perfectly acceptable if one's first reaction is puzzlement, of not knowing what to do – indeed it is far better to accept this puzzlement than to charge in with a tried and tested solution that is inappropriate.

- **Reflect on experience** – once people have recognized that there is a problem, they need to be able to reflect on it, to compare it with past experience.

- **Experiment with new approaches** – the crux of the reflective practitioner's competence lies in being able to reframe the problem and create new, alternative solutions.

Skills like these are complex. People must develop and hone them over time, in the workplace, with the support of experienced practitioners who can help them reflect on and learn from the experience. It is for this reason that approaches to development such as workplace coaching and mentoring are so crucial. And these require major investment from the organization to ensure that everyone has access to the support they need.

This is not to deny an important role to group learning. Indeed, group learning is likely to become even more important. But this is group learning, not where people sit in a room and are taught, but where they learn from each other in a facilitated manner. The new group learning calls for some important decisions, particularly around who will make up the groups. What will best be learned in the immediate team? What might best be learned by bringing people together from across the organization? And what may best be learned by bringing together a slice of the organization, cutting right through the hierarchy so that directors, managers, professionals, and support staff all sit down together and thrash things out.

Some questions

- *How many people in your organization are reflective practitioners? Who are they? How did they become good at it?*

- *What will it cost to carry on with the current training program? Which alternative approaches will be lost as a consequence? Can you afford the opportunity cost?*

- *Who are the people who can act as coaches and mentors in your organization? How can they create the time to coach and mentor? And how will they be supported themselves?*

- *Which combinations of people are likely to generate the most effective group learning?*

Advanced information handling skills – sharing, filtering, and adding meaning

So what does it boil down to? Basically, that although individuals and technologies and inventions will push the information age forward, it is organizations that will play the main part in shaping its destiny.

It is our belief that the organizations that will still be around and succeeding in 10 years' time will be those that gather the information available to them, use it, and continue to use it. The technology runs on apace, but people stay distressingly the same. And an organization needs to work on both the people and the technology to really make the most of the opportunities.

A new set of roles

- Organizations need to help everyone to rethink their roles in the organization.

- IT specialists need to come out of their cubby holes and learn to communicate and meet customer needs.

- Information hoarders need to share it.

- Everyone needs to look at how they add value and meaning to information.

- We all become little pocket-sized information champions. All taking responsibility for sharing information.

And leave the filing cabinets unlocked where possible.

We value it.

Importantly, the organization does not encourage the notion that anyone knows all that they can or should. It needs to understand and value expertise and experience but not reward people who remain stuck in their ways – unplugged.

Appropriate reward systems

We looked at this earlier but getting the right reward system is likely to be a lever that helps at an organizational level.

The purpose of reward systems is to reward people for helping the organization achieve its objectives.

Such a statement seems self-evident. But in practice reward systems can actually run counter to organizational policy and strategy. The traditional pay structure, linked closely to hierarchy, no longer fits with the new information organization.

As organizations face up to the challenge of managing information, it is essential that they consider how they can reward people for supporting the corporate objectives of sharing, filtering, and adding meaning.

In the first place, the overall reward structure must accommodate the increased importance of knowledge workers. Reward systems often straightjacket people into a particular career path. Information organizations must avoid this trap. Taking the line of Don Tapscott and Art Caston,

Don Tapscott
and Art Caston,
*Paradigm Shift:
The New
Promise of
Information
Technology*

> Rather than discouraging or killing the development of professional competency by promoting professionals to become managers, the new enterprise provides professional career paths and programs in which a professional can be as, or more, senior than managers. Individual contributors are rewarded based on competency and accomplishment rather than span of control.

And part of the reward should be time to go out there and learn. The following gives a flavor of the way things are changing.

■ Developing internal consultants

Increasingly human resource specialists within organizations are having to rethink their roles. The traditional HR department, discrete from the rest of the organization, seems out of step with the changing times. Several HR teams are developing their staff into a new role where they work closely with managers in client sections of the organizations.

In the process, HR staff are moving from jobs such as training manager or personnel assistant into the much broader role of internal consultant – a form of knowledge worker. They act as suppliers – of knowledge, expertise, and advice – to their internal customers. The learning curve is steep, as people leave a comfortable niche and have to develop the competences required to become immediately responsive to client needs. But the benefits are considerable as consultants are able to meet client needs more directly and effectively.

A traditional reward structure is inappropriate to such internal consultants, whose professional competence and value to the organization may become as important, if not more so, than that of the managers they serve. New reward structures based on competence are needed. One organization, for example, has carefully mapped the competences likely to be required as their internal consultants become established and start to take a more proactive and responsible role. These competences form the basis for staff development, but they also link directly into the new salary structure. As people become more competent, so they can expect to see their salary increase.

But it's possible to go further than this. The reward system can contain incentives that reward information sharing. An organization may consider offering learning awards for the biggest contribution to helping the company's information capacity to grow.

In real life

We have talked a lot about envisioning and the way things should, and indeed might, be. But how are real organizations modeling themselves to take real advantage of the information age?

■ Closer to the customer – the challenge for out-of-town retailing

The growth of massive out-of-town stores creates a major challenge for the big retail chains. Superstores can offer cost savings, higher throughput, and greater profits. But how do you stay close to your customers?

One answer, developed in the UK by Tesco, is the loyalty card. To the customer, a loyalty card offers a new payment method, with savings for large and repeat purchases. To the retailer it offers the scope to gain and retain customer loyalty.

But the loyalty card offers new opportunities too. It gives the retailer the scope to capture detailed information about customer spending habits. Stores will be able to track when individual shoppers visit, what they buy, and so forth.

If stores can effectively manage this information, it offers enormous scope for individual promotions, developing product lines that high-spending customers like, and responding to changes in customer-spending patterns.

If organizations are to make the most of these exciting opportunities, then everyone must get better at sharing, filtering, and adding meaning.

Organizations can help make this happen by putting systems in place like datawarehousing and by working on a number of softer skills.

■ From push to pull – managing knowledge at Hewlett Packard

The development of "just-in-time" manufacturing in Japan created a major shift in how production lines worked. Instead of pushing work down the line, with the risk of swamping people and failing to spot errors, the just-in-time approach asks workers to pull work in as and when they need it.

One of the key problems around information management is the push mentality. We are swamped by information which arrives when we least need it. To tackle the problem, Hewlett Packard Corporate Information Systems has introduced a pull approach to knowledge distribution. They put key documents onto Web or Lotus Notes systems. People can then access the information when they need it.

Meanwhile, the Knowledge Management Group brings in information about the process of generating products from across the company. They add value by identifying, editing, and formatting material so that it is easier to access and use, and share the information with other people via a Web-based system called Knowledge Links.

And finally ... almost

That is very nearly that.

In this chapter we looked at some of the ways organizations can keep up with the information age. But really the age will be a partnership between organization and individual.

And the organization of the future may look very similar to the one we have today or indeed very different. Back in the 1960s McLuhan and Fiore pointed out that:

> "the new electronic interdependence recreates the world in the image of a global village."

Maybe, but there are still plenty of skyscrapers and fewer and fewer villages.

M. McLuhan
and G. Fiore,
*The Medium is
the Massage*

References

Adams, P., Conway, M. and Owens, N. *The Strategic Use of Information Systems and Technology*, NHSTD, 1992.

Edwards, C., Ward, J. and Bytheway, A. *The Essence of Information Systems*, Prentice Hall, 1991.

Eskin, F. "Daydream believers," in *Health Service Journal*, 102:5319 (1992).

Handy, C. *The Age of Unreason*, Business Books, 1989.

McLuhan, M. and Fiore, G. *The Medium is the Massage* (*sic*), Penguin Books, 1967.

Morgan, G. *Images of Organization*, Sage, 1986.

Mumford, E. *Designing Participatively*, Manchester Business School, 1983.

Pedler, M., Burgoyne, J. and Boydell, T. *The Learning Company*, McGraw Hill, 1991.

Schön, D. *The Reflective Practitioner: How Professionals Think in Action*, Basic Books, 1983.

Sheaff, R. and Peel, V. (eds). *Managing Health Service Information Systems*, Open University Press, 1995.

Tapscott, D. and Caston, A. *Paradigm Shift: The New Promise of Information Technology*.

understanding the language: some words and ideas explained

This section explains some words and concepts associated with the information age. We begin with some longer pieces on issues of interest.

■ Convergence

What is the point in gossip if you can't share it? Similarly, what is the point in information if it remains stored on one computer accessible only by the person who put it there. It is this basic human need for sharing data and information across organizations and, despite evidence to the contrary, government departments, that has finally released the true power of computing. The growth of networking technology is the enabler behind the so-called information age, or to be considerably more accurate, the information access age.

It is now essential for any IT department to be as closely concerned with the physical shifting of data as it is with the development of processing power. This blurring of the lines between telecoms and computing has resulted in the growing convergence of two traditionally very different industries with completely different cultures – forcing both cooperation and increased competition.

But what effect will the outcome of this convergence have for consumers and the telecoms and computing industries? For the consumer it represents reduced costs and the seamless shift from stand alone technology to true networked computing via the Internet and Intranets. For the computer industry it creates opportunities as suppliers to the telecoms industry while also expanding the potential of their own products. For the global telecoms business however, it is both a threat and an opportunity. As they become increasingly reliant on technology to manage networks and switches they run the risk of becoming mere bit shifters, providing just the infrastructure to carry data while not adding any value to the services they provide.

The shifters of data face a squeeze on profits both from regulators and from increased competition from new entrants such as on-line service providers and Internet access companies. Moreover, the potential for additional revenue mostly lies with the people who create the data and own the rights to that data. To address this threat telecoms companies are already building new computer-driven intelligent networks to offer a wider range of value added services. However, regulatory constrictions currently prevent telecoms companies from taking advantage of their superiority in infrastructure whereas competitors such as cable are free to eat at their markets for data and voice transmissions, while at the same time offering additional service such as broadcast and interactive consumer products.

The rapid increase in other forms of digital transmissions using co-axial, satellite, fiber optic, and wireless systems will enable massive amounts of new bandwidth to be delivered across all sectors. This will further the convergence of the digital age, not just between telecoms and technology but also bring the entertainment and information providers to the party. The future will be one of joint skills, partnerships and alliances. It will not be enough to show competence in one sector only. This is particularly true for the telecoms industry if it is not to be marginalized and ultimately seen as no more important than the woman or man who delivers the mail.

■ Internet Access: On-line companies and service providers

With the dramatic increase in awareness of the commercial opportunities of the Internet, more and more companies are scrambling to provide connectivity and hook into the perceived profit machine that the Internet had apparently become. These suppliers range in size from global on-line companies such as CompuServe and Prodigy, with customer bases in the millions, through the larger Internet service providers such as Demon in the UK, down to small service providers giving access to the local area only – this would include companies such as Powernet which provides access to just the Milton Keynes area in the UK.

The on-line companies were the first to provide simple, but closed, access to the wider community outside academia and the military. These services, though responsible for attempting the earliest commercial efforts to utilize the power of network-based services, provided a reasonably user-friendly interface but lacked the global resources of the Internet. As access to the Internet has become progressively easier over the past few years, it was inevitable that the on-line companies, faced with the erosion of their customer base and the simplicity of the World Wide Web, would have to provide open access to the Internet in parallel with their closed group services. This strategy has proved remarkably successful and in fact 40 per cent of all US Internet traffic flows through America Online's network.

Internet service provision has proved one of the growth industries of the 1990s and, as with all good tales of the computer industry, was and indeed still can be, very much a garage operation. There are estimated to be over 600 service providers in the US alone and the global figure exceeds over 1,000. However, the entry of major players such as the public telephone networks, including BT, and major hardware and software companies, such as IBM and Microsoft, all competing aggressively for market share will make maintaining profit levels and competing on service increasingly difficult for even the largest players in the sector. This will be particularly true of the more mature markets in the US and Europe.

For the moment though, this is all good news for the consumer, and provided that capacity can match growth, the continual driving down of access costs should continue for some time to come. More competition and growth is likely to be fueled by major content owners including record companies, film studios, and publishers keen to maximize the commercial exploitation of their products. Leading content owners such as Berttelsmann in Germany, Japan's Sony, and News Corporation are already heavily involved.

It is this commercial exploitation that will ultimately be crucial if real long-term value is to be extracted from the Internet and other on-line environments. For the Internet service providers and on-line companies their key advantage lies in their proven ability to provide access. The challenge lies in whether they have the ability to transform themselves into managers of content provision, and creating the billing and customer services necessary to satisfy demand.

Major companies

In 1966 the biggest computer company in the world was IBM, in 1996 the biggest computer company in the world is - you've guessed it, IBM. So not much change there. However, the reality is somewhat different. While IBM in terms of turnover still remains the biggest company, its preeminent position has been under attack for a number of years. It has gone from being the dominant company in terms of standards, hardware, and software to now being just another computer company.

The history of "Big Blue," as IBM is popularly known, stretches back to 1890 when a forerunner under Herman Hollerith was commissioned by the US government to build a machine to collate data from the US Census. But it wasn't until 1924, under Thomas J. Watson, that the company changed its name to International Business Machines and gradually established a preeminence in technology and innovation that would not be seriously challenged until the late 1980s.

The challenge, when it did come was from an unlikely source, the introduction of IBM's hugely successful personal computer in 1983 ironically created the opportunity for a host of other companies (both software and hardware) to enter the market. Hardware manufacturers such as Compaq introduced what were then known as IBM-compatible machines, these machines were often superior to IBM's own equipment and cheaper. Despite maintaining pole position in the mainframe market, the attack on the personal computer sector which IBM, with monolithic arrogance had come to regard as its own, proved almost fatal to the company.

In other areas too IBM proved incapable of adjusting to the new reality of the technology industry. The decision by IBM to use under license the operating system for the IBM PC is regarded as one of the most short-sighted decisions in the history of corporate management. Instead of developing its own operating system it used the then tiny Microsoft Corporation's MS DOS system for the personal computer. The unproved and unknown Bill Gates transformed Microsoft into a global software giant and left IBM in a position of increasing weakness reliant on narrow focus hardware production.

Real profitability moved from hardware into the more esoteric world of software development and the marketing of software applications. Ever cheaper hardware imports, particularly from the Far East, cut inroads into IBM's position. Microsoft and other software companies had developed a reason to own a computer. From spread sheets to word processing and, of course, operating systems, software companies became the cool kids on the block, beloved of stock analysts worldwide.

And for the future? The challenge for Microsoft could easily come from newcomers Netscape with their World Wide Web browser software which was launched onto the market in the mid-nineties. Led by Mark Andresson and Jim Clark ex-CEO of Silicon Graphics, the flotation of Netscape, despite the misgivings of many in the industry, captured the imagination and on release day the share price leapt making instant millionaires of the founders. Software is king, hardware like the cables that carry electricity, is just another utility.

The Internet

Whenever the Internet is described, and there are almost as many ways of describing the Net as there are companies and people anxious to join in the fun, one thing remains constant. It has changed the way in which we perceive and use technology. The personal computers on desktops and attached to office networks, are now more than just useful devices to tap out letters, draft budgets, impress the boss, oh and play games. In fact, the PC and the intelligence that PCs represent via the Internet are probably the most important developments in communications since the postage stamp was invented.

This is almost despite the Internet's origins. During the mid-sixties an ambitious US Government Cold War project was created to develop secure communications in the event of nuclear attack. These early, top secret experiments, with the objective of connecting just a couple of nodes (or computers) have paved the way for easily accessible and cheap worldwide communications and a range of spin-off products and services. It has also created a burgeoning multi-billion dollar commercial opportunity driven by continuous technological innovation. The most important of which so far is the World Wide Web, which replicates the point and click simplicity of today's operating systems such as Mac OS and Windows 95.

But what is the Internet? At its simplest, the Internet is a global network of open computer networks communicating primarily via standard telephone connections and speaking the same language (Transmission Control Protocol/Internet Protocol which can be installed on any machine). The networks which make up the Internet belong to government departments, universities, corporations such as IBM, and commercial on-line systems such as Compuserve and Europe On-Line. Regardless of the oppressive hype, the scale of the Internet is truly phenomenal: over 30 million people have access to the Internet through over 3 million computers.

In the last few years, as commercial organizations have begun to realize the importance and financial opportunities associated with the Net, connection, which until recently was still the preserve of the experienced user, has become relatively straightforward. Most Internet service providers (such as Demon or Planet On-Line) supply ready to load software and are rapidly improving levels of customer care to cater for the novice user. With simplicity of access and use comes increased growth and while current use of the Internet is still dominated by e-mail and information retrieval, the future of Net use is considerably more complex and exciting.

Already, low-quality voice and video are possible and, as bandwidth and speed of access increases, these uses are likely to provide a quantum leap unimagined just 20 years ago. PCs or the TV set in the corner, will provide access to a bewildering array of services and functions and the Internet, and models based around the technology used, will become as ubiquitous as the telephone is today. In fact distributed intelligence (the Internet) is likely to become the model for the future of all electronic communication - embraced by telecom operators and technologists throughout the world.

Databases

Just how much information is out there? The whole world is a vast repository of raw data. In fact, we are awash in it. These days it is barely possible to walk down the street without tripping over a wayward pile of the stuff. The trouble is so much of it is like a kid's football team – a confused mass – with the object of the game, the football, only occasionally visible among a melee of legs and high-pitched screams. If it could only be organized perhaps something useful could be made of it.

That, of course, is exactly what a database tries to do. A database is an attempt to organize and transform raw material into something effective and profitable. Take a telephone directory, imagine if you knew that the name you wanted to find was definitely in the book but the information available was completely unstructured. It is immediately apparent that data without order is almost worthless.

It is wrong of course to assume that we suddenly have more information. It has always been there. Governments and businesses are by their very nature bureaucratic. In Tudor times the Elizabethan secret service collated vast amounts of data on the Virgin Queen's subjects and enemies. Any business worth its salt would think a day incomplete if a few forms had not been filled out and filed. Sales dockets, delivery notes, coffee-making rotas are all vital ingredients in the running of a successful office.

But then what? While it is very nice to have lots of data hanging around filling up shelves and making manufacturers of filing cabinets happy, there will always come a time when some bright, eager to get on type, will want to impress the boss by using some of that information for something useful. Access then becomes a problem – delving through ten years of dusty files, however well organized, is never going to be fun.

Today it is different. From the time when Herbert Hollerith was commissioned by the US government to mechanize the 1890 census, achieving access to data has progressively become easier and is now adding value rather than adding expense as a storage item. The organization of information, from the details of a window cleaner's round, to the entire contents of Encyclopedia Brittanica, can now be organized effectively and intelligently using tools developed over the last three decades for that specific purpose.

From recording sales patterns to ensuring that leads are not missed, data is organized and refined in a multiplicity of ways. A supermarket uses databases to manage stock control, understanding customer needs and maximizing profit. The Internet – the world's biggest database – is a vast repository of information that has always existed but now, instead of being contained in libraries around the world, and without generous travel expenses mostly unreachable – is not only easily accessible but, and perhaps more importantly, unlike the disorganized telephone book, can be sorted and output in a way most useful to the user.

Operating Systems

In 1995, after much delay, Microsoft, following the largest marketing campaign ever seen, finally launched Windows 95. This much hyped successor to Windows 3.1 made the development and launch of operating systems seem positively glamorous. Why? After all an operating system – the software that tells your computer how to run itself – doesn't exactly have the whizz bang excitement of a fully fledged multimedia product with moving pictures, text, and a full chorus line of dancers. The trouble is, without an operating system your computer is about as useful as a car without an engine.

The fact is the operating system market is huge – in fact, it's bigger than that – it is positively gigantic. In the coming year it is estimated that over 50 million personal computer units will be shipped. At present Microsoft dominates this market. Although there are other operating systems – some of which, particularly Apple's system 7.5.3 offering significant advantages and of which earlier versions was the first on the block as far as using a graphical interface is concerned – Microsoft's Windows has benefited massively from it's early association with the development of the IBM PC XT in the eighties.

In the days when IBM set de facto standards for the computing world, the launch of the PC XT required other manufacturers – partly to satisfy customer insistence – to build machines that were IBM compatible. This meant using the same operating system – DOS and later MS/DOS. With considerable foresight, and a small measure of good fortune, Microsoft CEO Bill Gates, despite receiving the original commission from IBM, was free to sell his operating system to any other manufacturer.

IBM, believing itself to be a builder of machines, failed to understand that the future, and also one of the major profit drivers of technology, lay with software. This lack of foresight ranks as probably one of the greatest corporate errors of all time. However, IBM was not alone in misreading the future. Apple, with an operating system that was both intuitive and, more importantly, more fun than MS/DOS or Windows 3.1, refused to license its own operating system to other manufacturers.

Apple believed it could dominate both sides of the market – the manufacture of both hardware and software. It was hardly likely that the global market place was going to fall for that old trick! It was equally unlikely that Microsoft was going to let Apple dominate the graphic user interface market. The use of icons to communicate with a computer, and the notion of a screen desktop (the interface) was swiftly imitated by Microsoft.

Both Apple and IBM have faced an uncertain future in the last few years. Both have undergone radical surgery in a belated attempt to keep up, but Microsoft continues to expand and maintain a dominant position in both the operating system and applications marketplace. Can anybody challenge this domination? Within the same marketplace, probably not. But the marketplace changes. The Internet and the possible advent of network computing are already raising questions. As with IBM and Apple, the challenge may be more than even Microsoft can meet.

Hardware

While humans, perhaps mirroring the demise of the dinosaur, continue to grow bigger and, judging by the amount of heart disease, more lethargic, the technology we have created and continue to engineer becomes ever faster, ever smaller and ever better. And with the advent of nanotechnology, it is almost possible to imagine the creation of something so small and fast that it probably won't even have the time to exist at all.

It is almost impossible to look at the development of computing machines without looking in parallel at the matching progress in software. However, to establish what drives what is a striking example of the chicken and egg situation. Is the machine developed to take advantage of improved software or is software developed to capitalize on improvements in hardware architecture. The answer is that it is probably a mixture of the two. Both elements are fundamental to improvements in computing power and neither can exist in splendid isolation.

Commonly reckoned to be the father of modern computing is Charles Babbage. His invention in 1834 of the Analytical Engine is regarded as the first example of the digital computer. The machine was controlled by punch cards which effectively constituted the first software program. This, and subsequent purely mechanical attempts at producing engines or machines to assist with complex calculations, helped to pave the way for the development by the early part of the twentieth century of the first electromechanical devices.

By the late thirties valves, originally developed for the radio industry, allowed machines to work at several thousand times faster than the earlier mechanical relays. By the Second World War both the Germans and the Allies were working on the creation of large-scale machines to assist the war effort. In Germany, Zuser failed to convince the Nazi high command of the relevance of his machine the Z1, but in the US experimentation with the valve led to the creation of ENIAC – Electronic Numerical Integrator and Calculator. A monster of a machine weighing over 30 tons.

Within the context of the times, ENIAC's processing power was enormous. But by today's standards ENIAC can be regarded as having the processing power of a fountain pen. However, in 1947 with the invention of the transistor, the computer age as we now understand it began to take off.

Semiconductor technology now enables thousands of circuits to be etched onto small chips. In fact, a recent announcement from a leading company indicates that soon it will be possible to place millions of circuits onto tiny boards. Today the average household convenience is probably capable of handling a moon landing. As basic hardware has become smaller so too has it also become more powerful. But the development cycle is not over. The battle to produce ever faster and smaller machines continues. Unless some method of thought transference to operate the machines of the future can be devised – perhaps the genetic future for mankind will have to be smaller fingers.

short words: big meanings

Accounting package: Software developed to automate the accounting function of businesses of all sizes. Accounting software has proved one of the great enablers for the growth of the information access age.

Acronym: Beloved of technologists everywhere. Acronyms (the creation of a word by taking the first letter of a collection of words such as RISC – Reduced Instruction Set Computing) are an attempt to make sure outsiders are kept in the dark.

Active cell: The current position of the cursor in a spreadsheet.

Adobe Illustrator: One of the leading design software packages for illustrators and graphic designers.

AIX: Advanced Interactive Executive. One of a number of versions of the UNIX operating system.

Aldus PageMaker: Launched in 1985, Aldus Pagemaker was the first page layout software for PCs. It remains a market leader to this day.

Alpha test: The first of a series of debugging and testing operations for new software. This would normally be limited to developers working within the confines of the developing company.

Apple: One of the most creative companies to come out of California. Apple was the first company to use a graphical user interface for personal computers. Its range of Macintosh computers helped to revolutionize the design industry (see Aldus Pagemaker).

Application: A computer program designed to meet a particular purpose. (See accounting package.)

Architecture: The physical design and construction of a computer.

ARPANET: Advanced Research Projects Agency Network. Developed by the US Department of Defense Advanced Research Projects Agency as a means of connecting university and government department computers to enable secure communication in the event of nuclear war. ARPANET paved the way for the development of the Internet.

Artificial intelligence: The still unproven desire to create computers which are able to learn and mimick human intelligence.

ASCII: American Standard Code for Information Interchange. Created in 1968, it changes letters, numbers, and symbols into a seven-bit code to enable the interchange of data between different products.

AT&T: American Telephone and Telegraph Company. The giant American telecoms carrier. AT&T competes head to head with other national carriers around the world in the massive international data communications market.

Backup: The one thing everybody should do to ensure important data is not held at just one location, i.e. copying data from a PC to a disk.

Bandwidth: The type and range of frequencies that can be carried on a cable.

BASIC: Beginners All purpose Symbolic Instruction Code. A programming language developed in 1965.

Baud rate: The speed or measure of amount of data that can be transmitted along a communications line every second. Fax machines commonly transmit at 9,600 bits per second while modems for a PC transmit up to 38,000 bits per second.

Beta site/test: Following an internal alpha test new software is commonly sent to selected sites for a secondary test. This is designed to reveal bugs and problems apparent to the user rather than the developer.

Big Blue: The not altogether affectionate term for IBM. It refers to IBM's corporate color scheme.

Binary system: The common system used throughout computing. Binary works to a base of two rather than the decimal base of 10. The use of binary enables the representation of numbering to be reduced to a series of ones and zeros or, more simply, on and off.

Browser: (*See* Search engine.)

Bug: An error in a computer program. The term was coined by a developer who discovered that a moth had caused a malfunction in a relay panel of an early computer.

Bulletin board: Public and private information services. Accessed by computer and modem it is most often a cheap and unregulated method of obtaining pornography.

Byte: Binary Digit Eight. One of the least attractive and unrecognizable acronyms. A byte is an expression for one character or letter.

CAD: Computer Aided Design or Drafting. Software developed to automate elements of both engineering and architecture design.

CD: An optical storage device with a capacity of up to 700 megabytes of data.

Chip: The term synonomous with today's technology. A chip is an integrated circuit most usually made from silicon – from which the additional term of California's Silicon Valley also arose.

Client/Server: Network linking technology that has almost become the corporate world's holy grail. It was supposed to sign the death knell of mainframes by allowing small systems running different applications to communicate with and share information across all platforms.

Clone: Originally used in reference to manufacturers building machines compatible with early IBM machines such as the XT.

Compaq: One of the top ten computer manufacturers in the world. Compaq's revenue according to *Datamation* magazine for 1995 was in excess of $10 billion.

CompuServe: A US based on-line service provider. CompuServe's service was originally closed, unlike the Internet which is open to all, but increasing pressure from the Net, and the ease and simplicity of Netscape, has forced CompuServe to offer open access to a wider environment.

Convergence: The bringing together of separate strands of the technological environment. In particular, it refers to the unifying of telecommunications and computing. Telecommunications is increasingly dependent on computer technology to function and computing is just as reliant on telecommunications to transfer data from machine to machine.

Copy protection: A means of preventing illegal copying and distribution of software.

CPU: Central Processing Unit. The big box that sits underneath your VDU – Visual Display Unit. This is the bit of your computer system that does all the hard work.

DAT: Digital Audio Tape.

Data: Whether raw or refined, data is the basic building block of information technology.

Database: Data, see above, is collated and refined using a database. Information, such as sales leads, is gathered together and can then be output in a way most useful to the business needs.

Data warehousing: Complete historical database of a company's business. Extremely expensive to create and maintain.

dBASE: One of the most popular database packages. Manufactured by the US company, Borland.

Desktop publishing: The design and production of anything from newsletters to newspapers. Packages such as PageMaker has made designers of us all. Unfortunately, most people do not seem aware of the need to combine the technology with at the very least some basic training in design.

Digital: Digital Equipment Corporation. US based company primarily specializing in large system technology.

Disk: Removable data storage device.

DOS/MSDOS: Disk Operating System. Developed by the then tiny Microsoft, DOS, and later MSDOS. Until the development of intuitive software using Graphics, such as Windows, DOS was the primary operating system for personal computers. The complexity of DOS probably did more to turn people off computing than make them converts.

Electronic mail (e-mail): The sending of messages via the Internet is probably the most popular aspect of world networking. This service accounts for a greater proportion of traffic on the Internet than any service.

Encryption: The encoding of data, particularly to ensure security during transmission from one computer to another. The usual method involves scrambling the bit patterns at source with the recipient holding the password or coding format to enable decoding.

Excel: Microsoft's very popular multiplatform spreadsheet package.

Fiberoptics: The great hope of the digital future. Information can be transmitted at speeds vastly in excess of that achieved using standard copper-wire telephone connections.

File: In much the same way that an office filing cabinet is organized, data on a computer is held in a hierarchical system organized into files.

Font: The representation of letters and numerals of one particular size and style.

Fujitsu: The second largest in terms of revenue, computer manufacturer in the world. Japan based Fujitsu has major holdings in most major countries including the UK where it has a majority shareholding in ICL.

Gates (Bill): The CEO of software giant Microsoft. Successfully capitalized on the development of DOS to create a company that is dominant in the supply of software packages, which includes Word and Excel, and operating systems with Windows.

Gigabyte: It is not so long ago that a gigabyte of storage was an impossible dream. Today however many PCs come with at least half a gigabyte of storage and it will not be long before PCs will come with a standard gigabyte and more.

Gray market: The importing of software and hardware from a source country – usually the US – into another country without the permission of the manufacturer.

Groupware: An interlocking set of applications designed to aid the flow of information throughout a company. Applications will include electronic mail, diaries, and work software such as spreadsheets and wordprocessing.

GUI: Graphical User Interface. A clumsy term for the most liberating element in computing. Instead of DOS and its C:/ instructions and commands, commands are made via a mouse by clicking on graphic representations of files and programs. Initially popularized by Apple, Windows 95 is Microsoft's version.

Hacker: The demon of computing. A hacker is someone who gains unauthorized access to a network.

Hard copy: The book you are reading is hard copy. Anything produced onto paper by a computer is referred to as hard copy.

Hardware: The physical components of a computer system. This covers everything from the screen to the CPU.

Hewlett Packard: Top ten computer and peripherals manufacturer based in Palo Alto, California. The company is reknowned for its sophisticated printer technology.

Host: A host computer is one that sits at the hub of a network. This machine will have available all the software functions that may be required by a number of users.

IBM: The behemoth that still bestrides the global technology industry. IBM can trace its history back to 1890, but first became known as IBM in 1924. Despite recent troubles, including registering a loss for the first time ever in 1993, the appointment of new CEO, Lou Gerstner, has seen consolidation and recovery.

Icon: An on-screen device to indicate to users instructions or access to programs and data.

Intel: Probably the dominant force in the production of microprocessor technology – the term "Intel Inside" has almost become a de facto standard. Intel is representative of the typical start small grow huge story so common in the computer industry. Started in 1968 with 12 employees, the company now employs over 25,000 globally.

Interactive: The two-way exchange of information between computer and user.

Internet: The network of networks. Originally developed by the US Department of Defense to provide secure communications in the event of nuclear war. The development of the World Wide Web and browsers such as Netscape brought the Internet into the public conscience. There are now over 30 million users around the world.

Intranet: A private company network based around the same technology as the Internet.

ISDN: Integrated Services Digital Network. Making use of current telecom networks, ISDN enables the high-speed transmission of digital information – this can include video, voice, and data.

ISO: International Organization for Standardization. This body has responsibility for setting international standards to promote easier exchange of goods and services.

Jobs (Steve): The enfant terrible of computing. A highly opinionated and also very talented computer developer, he was co-founder of Apple and led the development of Apple's Macintosh range.

Kilobyte: A thousand bytes.

Keyboard: The standard interface between user and computer – other than the mouse.

LAN: Local Area Network. A small network connecting all machines and printers within a local environment. The use of a LAN allows users to share resources such as printers, software, and data.

Logon: Password protection for networks and other systems allowing multi-use. The user to gain access must first enter the password.

Lotus: Lotus product 1-2-3 was one of the first spreadsheet packages to hit the market. It is still a highly popular package though the company itself is now owned by IBM.

Mainframe: The biggest machines in the family of computers. Although the processing power of todays PCs far exceed that of early mainframes, they can still be differentiated by the enormous processing and data management power they offer. Often a whole company's computer needs will be run from a mainframe.

Megabyte: A million bytes.

Memory: Usually refers to the available memory to run applications. For instance Microsoft Windows needs at least five Megabytes of RAM (Random Access Memory) just to be able to run.

Microsoft: Seattle-based Microsoft is one of the biggest software developers and publishers in the world. Led by CEO, Bill Gates, Microsoft dominates the market for operating systems with it's Windows 95 product.

MIS: Management Information System. Utilising data collected throughout a company, information necessary to the deeper understanding of a company's performance can be extracted and analyzed.

MIT: Massachusetts Institute of Technology. One of the foremost technology thinktanks in the world.

Modem: Modulator–Demodulator. A device that enables the communication between digital devices. It converts digital data to analogue to allow standard telephone (which transmits analogue signals) connections to transmit the data.

Mouse: Along with the keyboard, the mouse is the user's main method of communicating instructions to a computer. The mouse came into its own with the development of Apple's point and click graphical user interface.

Multimedia: The combining of a multiplicity of environments to the user, This can include video, sound, communication, and text.

Netscape: The most popular browser for the Internet. Netscape Corporation, led by Mark Andresson, developers and publishers of Netscape have achieved a dominant market position which is unlikely to be troubled in the near future.

Network: A collection of computers working together, sharing information and applications. There is a number of different acronyms including WAN – Wide Area Networks, LAN – Local Area Network used to describe the size and complexity of the network.

Newsgroups: Internet-based gatherings of people with similar interests. This can range from Cricket or stampcollecting to things you most certainly wouldn't like your mother to know about.

NTT: Nippon Telegraph & Telephone. By a number of measures Japan's NTT is regarded as the largest company in the world. Recent restructuring, however, has been designed to cut staff and enable NTT to compete in the global marketplace for data communications.

Novell: One of the major suppliers of networking software.

Objects: Reusable software modules – such as icons, images, functions etc. – which can be given specific attributes and relationships and can adapt to change. These can significantly reduce software development time.

On-line: Similar to the Internet, on-line services such as CompuServe or America On-Line offer a comprehensive range of services within a closed environment. Increasingly, however, these closed services are having to provide access to the wider Internet.

Open systems: Computer networks designed to conform to standards which will allow different types of hardware and software systems to interact.

Operating system: A program, usually supplied preloaded with a computer, that provides all of the basic control functions to manage the running of all other programs – such as word processing or spreadsheets. Well known operating systems include Apple's System 7.5.3 and Microsoft's Windows 95.

OEM: Original Equipment Manufacturer. A company which supplies unbadged equipment for badging by value-added resellers.

OSF: Open Software Foundation. A group set up by several of the world's leading vendors to encourage and promote specifications for an open software environment.

Packet switching: The core of Internet development is the use of packet switching. Rather than send whole chunks of data at one time through one source, data is split into packets with each element able to find its own way through a multiplicity of sources to its destination.

PC or Personal Computer: The name given to any computer not dependent for processing power on any other source. It is closely associated with the term desktop computing.

Pentium: Intel's microprocessor which replaced the Intel 486. This new processor has a third more transistors than the previous model.

Pixel: The smallest element that makes up a computer-generated graphics picture as displayed on the VDU.

Postscript: A programming device used to interpret how an image or font will be printed.

Program: An ordered set of instructions to enable the computer to carry out a specific task or tasks. Programs, also known as software, include word processing packages and spreadsheets.

Programming language: Software, such as word processing packages, are written using a programming language. There is a wide range of languages including C and C++.

Protocol: To enable computers to talk to each other, i.e. via a modem, each computer must use the same protocol, e.g. TCP/IP.

PTN: Public Telephone Network. Also known as TOs, Telcos, etc.

Quark Xpress: The main rival to PageMaker as the preferred page layout software package. In recent years its popularity has outstripped that of PageMaker.

Qwerty: The name given to the standard keyboard used throughout the world. The name refers to the six letters at the top left of the first letter row. Despite the inefficient placing of letters, there have been no real attempts to change the layout.

RAM: Random Access Memory. This aspect of a computers memory contains only the program in use. It is volatile and dependent on power to function. Hence, the need to regularly save work in progress.

RDBMS: Relational Database Management System. A database management system that achieves flexibility in establishing relations between different aspects of data contained in a database.

ROM: Read Only Memory. Unlike the volatile RAM, ROM cannot be overwritten. For example CD ROM, the data contained on the CD is meant to be permanent. Data stored cannot be lost if there is a power failure.

Rightsizing: Depending on one's outlook, it either means an attempt by an organization to find computer solutions to fit current needs or, to the more cynical, an attempt by a organization to reduce costs by cutting staff.

RISC: Reduced Instruction Set Computing. The reduction use of instructions to command the computer to carry out various operations at a faster rate then previously achieved.

RSI: Repetitive Strain Injury. A term used to refer to a group of bodily complaints such as minor aches in wrists and shoulders, or a debilitating loss of use and feeling in the hands and arms, associated with repetitive tasks such as using a computer keyboard or working on a factory assembly line.

Scanner: An external device to enable the digitization of images to allow input to a computer.

SCSI: Small Computer System Interface. An interface standard developed to allow connection of peripheral devices (printers, scanners) to a computer.

Search engine: Commonly used to describe a command or query language developed to search databases, in particular the Internet. One of the most popular for Web users is Yahoo.

Shareware: Sotfware protected by copyright but distributed most often on trial basis. If the user likes it they are asked to forward a fee, usually minimal, to the developer.

Silicon Valley: Santa Clara Valley in California. So-called because of the preponderence of computer manufacturers and software developers in the area.

Software: Computer programs written to perform specific tasks – such as spreadsheets, database packages.

SOHO: Small Office, Home Office. With the advent of improved home communications and powerful personal computers, many people are taking advantage of these developments to either work independently from home or to continue working for a large corporation but carrying out their function in the home office.

Spreadsheet: One of the key packages in the development in popularity of personal and corporate computing. Spreadsheets are programs which allow the manipulation and management of data and are most commonly used in the presentation of accounts and associated management requirements.

Sun: Sun Microsystems. Not one of the top ten hardware manufacturers but an increasingly important one with particular regard to the development of the Internet. Sun Work Stations and Servers are regarded as the workhorses of Internet architecture.

Supercomputer: Basically a very big, very fast computer. A supercomputer sits at the top of the hierarchy of computing technology.

TCP/IP: Transmission Control Protocol/Internet Protocol. The key interface for the management and transmission of data over the Internet.

UNIX: Developed in 1971 by AT&T, UNIX is rapidly becoming one of the most popular operating systems.

User-friendly: A term widely used to describe anything that the novice user should find easy to use. In practice, of course, it has very little relevance to the real world. We have all seen video units described as user friendly!!

Virtual reality: The simulation by computer of events or tasks to enable training or role playing.

Virus: Not to be confused with Bug. A bug is an unforseen error in a program, whereas a virus is a set of instructions deliberately inserted onto a computer's hard disk or a software program. It can, if left untreated or undetected by one of the Antivirus software programs available, cause minor inconvenience, or in some cases major data loss and disruption.

WAN: Wide Area Network. Unlike Local Area Networks, WANs can be office to office, country to country.

Windows: Microsoft's incredibly popular operating system. Based loosely on Apple's operating system, it makes use of icons, images, and menus to create an intuitive atmosphere, in which the user is graphically shown options with which to issue commands to the computer.

World Wide Web: The World Wide Web, or WWW, provides a graphical interface to enable simple access to information available on the Internet. In terms of traffic and number of sites, it is the fastest growing element of the Internet.

Word processing: Along with, and probably more so than spreadsheets and accounting packages, word processing has proved the success story of computing. Word processing packages such as Microsoft's Word or WordPerfect enable the user to easily create, write, and change documents, letters, etc. for output to hard copy or transmission via a network.

WYSIWYG: What you see is what you get. The display on screen of how the output will appear in print.

index